"I met Captain Geoff Abbott shortly after flying a failed rescue mission attempting to save people trapped in the World Trade Center on 9/11. Prior to 9/11, I was a young Coast Guard Lieutenant who saw things that could be improved but felt powerless in a large organization to do anything about it. I was fortunate to have Capt. Abbott as my mentor. He shared his paper on 'Leading Change from the Middle,' which this book expands upon, and helped empower me by realizing we were all leaders at various levels of whatever organization we were in. His guidance and support helped me implement five agency-wide innovation projects and truly make a difference. I deployed with him to New Orleans immediately after Hurricane Katrina and while there, numerous people from throughout the Coast Guard came up to Capt. Abbott and thanked him for transforming their lives the same way he had transformed mine. This book will give you the tools needed to make a difference no matter what level you are in any organization."

Chris Kluckhuhn, Rescue Helicopter Pilot,
U.S. Coast Guard Reserve (Retired)
Coast Guard Annual Innovation Award Winner
Founder and CEO of Avwatch, Inc.

"Capt. Abbott makes public what has made many professional careers by recognizing that no one has a corner on the market of good ideas. The superior leader encourages idea generation from the troops actually doing the work and rewards those who identify a better way to accomplish the mission."

James Loy, Admiral, former Coast Guard Commandant,
TSA Administrator, and Deputy Secretary of the
Department of Homeland Security

"Like a twenty-five-dollar ax to save people trapped under roofs in rising flood waters, *Unauthorized Progress* breaks through the tangle of hierarchy and compliance cultures to liberate the human ingenuity needed to solve mission-stymying, real-world problems. From a platform of solid, often jaw-dropping decisions by individuals who hold themselves accountable for results, he builds a framework to help us think through when and how to take appropriate, responsible and 'unauthorized' initiatives."

Ira Chaleff, author of *Intelligent Disobedience:*
Doing Right When What You're Told to Do Is Wrong
and *The Courageous Follower*

"*Unauthorized Progress* provides a template for action for those seeking to achieve success and make a difference at any level. Geoff Abbott is an outstanding role model and mentor! His sage guidance will empower you to lead at any level. His methodical process will help you recognize opportunities to take charge even when you are not! He quantifies a 'never give up' strategy that gives you the strength to continue regardless of the obstacles. This is a must-read book for anyone, especially those who aren't privileged to have a mentor but who truly desire to break out of the ordinary and become a transformational leader."

Donna Barbisch, Major General, U.S. Army (Retired)

"*Unauthorized Progress* addresses what is often a fuzzy and potentially risky concept of leading beyond one's authority. Much like many of our nation's founding fathers, the inspiring stories and strategies about ordinary people striving to achieve meaningful results, often leads to extraordinary impacts. A process and supporting strategies for leading 'from the middle' are presented in a clear, logical, and convincing manner that shouts, 'You can do this!'"

Donald T. Phillips, author of *Character in Action*
and *The Founding Fathers on Leadership*

"Worth your time! This is applicable for people who work in both the military and the business world. Geoff has filled in the spaces around my personal leadership foundation, built at the Coast Guard, DHS, and DOD executive leader programs and at Harvard's National Preparedness Leadership Initiative. As workspaces grow in diversity, the need for books like this has never been more important to help create inclusive environments."

Cari Thomas, Rear Admiral, U.S. Coast Guard (Retired)
CEO, Coast Guard Mutual Assistance

"Both practical and passionate, Geoff Abbott believes that with the right strategies, tools, and support, anyone can lead from wherever they are—and helps you believe it too! Organizations willing to upend the traditional hierarchical pyramid and empower their frontline and mid-level employees to take initiative and blaze trails will more quickly solve complex workplace challenges and seize opportunities to better serve their customers, employees, and communities."

Ken Jennings, author of *The Serving Leader*

"Geoff Abbott's approach of addressing one of the key principles in effective character-driven leadership by 'Leading from the Middle' is an excellent resource for all levels, whether in a supervisory or followership role. The true leadership players who make things happen come from the middle."

Vince Patton,
8th Master Chief Petty Officer
of the Coast Guard (Retired)

"Written in a story-based format, *Unauthorized Progress* describes several events where initiation and action taken by employees at various levels of the organization led to problem solving and constructive change that would have otherwise not occurred. Geoff Abbott captures the essence of how these people, motivated by mission, sought to resolve issues and provides a helpful step-by-step flowchart to help you navigate the process. This book truly speaks to being a leader from wherever you are in the organization."

Cyndi (Crother) Laurin, Ph.D., author of *Catch!*,
The Rudolph Factor, Be A Frontline H.E.R.O., and
AMP Your Outcome! Founder of Guide to Greatness, LLC

"Unauthorized Progress is full of great examples of what happens when everyday people make common sense a common practice in the workplace and feel empowered to initiate constructive change. The lessons in this book will help any leader, at any level, make excellence a habit, rather than an exception."

Scott Winter, International Leadership Coach
CEO, Collaborative Commons

"Unauthorized Progress is truly inspirational as well as practical. I look forward to seeing its impact on public life and global leadership. Whether the reader's calling is crisis management, procurement, or technological innovation, she will find the takeaways vivid and strategy tips actionable."

Ilyse Veron,
Innovation Communications Strategy Consultant
Former Editor of *The Public Manager* and
Reporter for *The NewsHour* with Jim Lehrer

"What I appreciate so much about this resource is that it's not only an encouraging challenge and inspiring call to action; Geoff provides practical guidance, grounded in real-life experiences, and a step-by-step guide for leading from the middle. After all, *'we are all in the middle.'"*

John Riordan, Senior Consultant,
John Riordan Leadership & Organization Development
Coach, Excellence in Government Fellows (1999-2019)

"Geoff Abbott's book powerfully proves that leadership is not a popularity contest—it's clearly a credibility contest. And leadership isn't only the purview of those at the highest level of organizations. As you'll see from the core principles and memorable stories of this engaging book, you'll gain the insight and inspiration to serve from wherever you are in your organization. I highly recommend it!"

Barry Rellaford, coauthor of
A Slice of Trust and cofounder of CoveyLink,
Creators of *The Speed of Trust*

"An unauthorized progression is a best practice for any industry. Dr. Abbott brings to light real people with real stories that emerged as 'solution providers.' He reminds us to have the wherewithal to seek out and recruit ideas, information, and problem solving from innovators at all levels in an organization. Dr. Abbott addresses 'wicked problems' leading to 'wicked opportunities' encouraging readers to 'proceed until apprehended.' He encourages readers with skill sets, how-to's, strategies, and summaries to notice the people around us and give them a seat and a say at the table."

Cheryl Brown, DBA, RN, Lieutenant Colonel,
U.S. Army (Retired)
Experienced Combat Trauma Nurse

"Filled with the practical lessons of experience, reflection, and wisdom, this is a must-read book for both senior leaders and the next generation. Geoff Abbott takes a simple idea—leading from the middle—and shows how it is the key to cultivating a culture that produces both high impact and innovative leaders. Through great stories, he demonstrates how time after time these principles have been put into action. This is a long-needed leadership development course provided in a single place."

Ray Blunt, Executive and Excellence
in Government Fellows Coach (Retired)

"Captain Geoff Abbott's book will strike a strong and resonant chord with anyone frustrated by the inefficiencies of top-down bureaucracy and the seemingly endless obstructions to 'doing the right thing.' Rather than stifling rank-and-file innovation and creativity, top-level organizational leaders must constantly strive to empower those in the trenches at all levels—those most intimately familiar with the issues—to solve them. Unleashing and endorsing the creativity of those currently forced to pursue 'unauthorized progress' will improve not only institutional efficiency, but organizational morale as well. The brave souls 'leading from the middle' must be embraced and encouraged as they continually strive to improve things, often against the tide."

Stephen "Hoog" Hoogasian, Colonel,
U2 Pilot, Office of Irregular Warfare,
U.S. Air Force (Retired)

"Government colleagues who have followed retired Coast Guard Capt. Geoff Abbott's progress as he has steadfastly developed his 'Leading from the Middle' work will be thrilled when they read this brilliant result. Using illustrative stories (Hurricane Katrina response, ambushes in the mountains of Afghanistan, California wildfires, New England lighthouses and others), Geoff clarifies the dynamics that quash some innovative ideas while providing integrated questions, strategy, and tools you can use to move better ideas to successful implementation. Every constructive person who wants to make a difference from within the bureaucracy can benefit from this proof that difference-making does not depend on rank or grade."

Kitty Wooley, Career Federal employee (Retired)
Excellence in Government Senior Fellows Board of Leaders
Founder of Senior Fellows and Friends

"Captain Abbott *nails it*. Effective operational leaders know, the best observations and ideas often come from outside the wardroom and chief's mess. The value of 'leading from the middle' has been recognized by mandated special evolution briefs involving the entire team with all encouraged to speak up. Similarly, each watchstander carries responsibility for ensuring safety of the ship and crew, requiring initiative, leadership, the ability to question the status quo, and taking appropriate action when necessary. In my experience, more changes to regulations and operational protocol originate from the keen insight of those in 'the middle' than any other group. It's essential that formal leadership not throttle that contribution. Capt. Abbott explains why in an engaging read."

Jim Mongold, Captain,
Former Commanding Officer of USCGC VIGILANT,
U.S. Coast Guard (Retired)

"In today's complex world, organizations need courageous and committed individuals at every level to accept responsibility for the success of their organization's mission. Capt. Abbott's work provides the insight, guidance, and real-life examples needed by those wishing to make a positive difference in their organizations. *Unauthorized Progress* is essential reading for every individual passionate about the mission and the people they serve."

Walt Besecker, Federal Senior Executive (Retired)
Excellence in Government Fellows
Leadership Coach (Retired)

UNAUTHORIZED
PROGRESS

LEADING FROM THE MIDDLE

Stories & Proven Strategies
for Making Meaningful Impacts

Foreword by

ADMIRAL THAD ALLEN,

USCG (Retired)

CAPTAIN GEOFF ABBOTT

U.S. Coast Guard (Retired)

ISBN:
978-1-7347307-0-8 (paperback)
978-1-7347307-1-5 (ebook)

Library of Congress Control Number: 2020906133

First printing: May 2020
Printed in Burke, Virginia, USA by Geoff Abbott

The publisher has strived to be as accurate and complete as possible in the creation of this book.

The advice and strategies found within may not be suitable for every situation. This work is sold with the understanding that neither the author nor the publisher is held responsible for the results accrued from the advice in this book.

While all attempts have been made to verify information provided for this publication, the publisher assumes no responsibility for errors, omissions, or contrary interpretation of the subject matter herein. Any perceived slights of specific persons, peoples, or organizations are unintended.

For more information, visit www.GeoffAbbottLeadership.com.

For bulk book orders, contact Geoff Abbott at AbbottGL@aol.com.

A Special Gift from Geoff

Now that you have your copy of *Unauthorized Progress – Leading From the Middle*, you are equipped with the tools and strategies needed to effectively initiate and influence positive change in your organization or community and make meaningful impacts. As you apply the techniques described, you will develop increased confidence to tackle complex challenges and issues that matter to you, your team, and your organization.

I also created the *Unauthorized Progress (UP)* toolkit to make it easy for you to immediately apply leading from the middle strategies. It includes summaries of key topics and useful tools:

- Leading Change from the Middle process flowchart
- Criteria decision-makers use to evaluate initiatives
- Common reasons innovative ideas are not pursued
- Leading from the middle implementation strategies and when they are most effective
- Reasons change initiatives fail and mitigation strategies
- Templates you can copy and adapt for your personal initiatives:
  - SWOT Analysis, Importance versus Urgency matrix, Cause and Effect diagram
- Sample questions to engage stakeholders and learn their perspectives

While the *UP Toolkit* can be purchased, I'm making it available free to all readers to accelerate your ability to lead from wherever you are in your organization.

Go to http://GeoffAbbottLeadership.com/gift to register for your gift. As another gift you will also receive tips and further information from me to confidently lead *from the middle*. You may, of course, unsubscribe at any time.

I'm in your corner. Let me know if I can help further – you can do this!

Geoff

This book is for the exceptional Coast Guard women and men and the public servants with whom I've been honored to serve. As law enforcement; first responders; military; intelligence; and federal, state, and local government professionals, you steadfastly safeguard our communities and nation and inspire us with your commitment, integrity, courage, and effectiveness.

Table of Contents

List of Figures

List of Tables:

Foreword

When Geoff Abbott asked me to write the foreword to this book, I agreed immediately for several reasons. First, Geoff was a stalwart supporter of my innovation agenda, first as Coast Guard Chief of Staff and then again as Commandant. Many leaders have visions, few are able to harness to the imagination of a team to give that vision life. Geoff has always felt empowered to convert vision to practice, but also to seize the opportunity and degrees of freedom to drive change from his position in the organization. For that reason, I wasn't surprised at the title or the content of *Unauthorized Progress*.

Second, I've spoken to thousands of federal employees on the opportunity and need to innovate in the federal government. While I have made the case that you can drive change and innovate from any level in government, I inevitably get challenged by frustrated career employees that any success I've had was because of my rank and ability to demand or direct change. Not true! Any public servant can and should drive innovation and change, but with appropriate consideration of the governing frameworks for resource allocation and policy making, as Geoff points out.

Third, one of my personal axioms is that the *status quo* is an oxymoron. The universe is expanding. Each nanosecond creates a different world, and there is no reverse. Most information we act on is latent, and we don't know what we don't know. That condition should prompt us to understand that we should always assume there is information we don't or can't know. The enduring challenge of the "perceived status quo" should be an accepted practice of good leaders. For these reasons, writing this foreword was an easy "yes" for me.

Geoff's request prompted me to reflect on an op-ed I wrote on public service in 2011. It's worthy of another look.

> During my four decades of public service, I have worked with many amazing people—some heroes who have risked their lives to save others, some who have risen to the occasion during crises like the Gulf oil spill and Hurricane Katrina, and many who have quietly gone about the business of serving the public with great dedication day-in and day-out. I was born while my father was at sea on a Coast Guard cutter.
>
> In the current political climate and discourse over the national debt, we have done a poor job of distinguishing between the need for fiscal responsibility and the value of public service, which is enduring.
>
> While politicians necessarily haggle over policy, budgets, and the size of government, it is worth remembering that it does not serve any of us as Americans when government employees are denigrated or vilified. We all want the best government possible, and our aim should be to encourage, not discourage, bright, capable people from serving their fellow citizens.
>
> During Hurricane Katrina, the Coast Guard saved over 30,000 people. In the midst of last year's Gulf oil crisis, we had employees from the Food and Drug Administration checking on the safety of the seafood; scientists from the Environmental Protection Agency monitoring water quality and the impact of the oil on the beaches and marshes; workers from the Fish and Wildlife Service working day and night to protect the birds, turtles, and other sea life; members of the U.S. Geological Survey working technical issues related to controlling the well; and the National Oceanic and Atmospheric Administration providing key data on weather and environmental conditions.
>
> For sure, government work may be just a paycheck for some employees, and as in any organization, there are those who don't

quite cut it. There is no institution, whether governmental, or in the private and nonprofit sectors, where mistakes are not made. But the great majority of public servants I have known and worked with, whether at the local, state, or federal level, have been hardworking people who often sacrifice their own time and resources to make a meaningful contribution.

In many ways, government is a lot like oxygen. You are not necessarily aware of it until you need it and don't have it anymore.

Imagine what it would be like taking your children to school and finding no one there to teach them, calling 9-1-1 and having no one respond to your emergency, having no sanitation workers to pick up your trash, no one building or maintaining our roads, no one guarding our borders, no one manning our embassies abroad, or no one providing health care to our wounded warriors or sending out Social Security checks.

The truth is that each and every day, civil servants are finding solutions to serious problems, assisting Americans in need, keeping us safe, and advancing our national interests.

I have always felt that there is something distinct and noble about a lifetime of public service. Our democracy, our institutions, and our well-being depend on people with an unwavering loyalty and commitment to serve.

President John F. Kennedy eloquently spoke about the importance of our federal public servants in 1962, a description that is worth repeating. In JFK's view, public service was "a proud and lively career," and government workers were engaged in a high calling.

"The success of this government, and thus the success of our nation, depends in the last analysis upon the quality of our career services," Kennedy said. "In foreign affairs, national defense, science and technology, and a host of other fields, they face problems of unprecedented importance and perplexity. We are all dependent on their sense of loyalty and responsibility as well as their competence and energy."

President Kennedy had it right, and it would serve our nation well if more of us, along with our elected leaders today, provided the same kind of support and recognition to our civil servants. To my fellow public servants, thank you for your service.

In the face of recurring skepticism on the value of government service, the hollowing of the federal workforce, and associated lack of institutional memory, and the need for a government that can meet the ever-increasing challenges of a rapidly changing world, this book is well timed.

Its strategies apply beyond the public sector and our nation to all who serve others, including volunteers, the nonprofit community, and private sector from the local volunteer fire department to the international medical community urgently working to combat the outbreak and develop a vaccine for the coronavirus—local, regional and national health officials, hospitals, the scientific community, the World Health Organization, pharmaceutical companies, and many others.

We need leaders at all levels who can seize the opportunity to change their immediate world of work and inspire others to do the same. I can't say it any better than Arthur Ashe did. He said to achieve excellence, "Start where you are. Use what you have. Do what you can." Wise counsel that I have used my entire professional and personal life. Join me and Geoff.

Admiral Thad Allen,
23rd Commandant,
U.S. Coast Guard (Retired)

PREFACE

There's a way to do it better—find it.
- Thomas Edison

Unauthorized Progress provides effective strategies and insights you can immediately use to successfully implement constructive change. These strategies and insights are illustrated through inspirational true stories of ordinary people initiating or influencing action to achieve extraordinary contributions. Each of us can influence productive change and effectively lead "from the middle," e.g., beyond our "formal authority." This book recognizes the potential of talented and motivated people to successfully lead at any level and make a significant difference to their organization, community, cause, or people they serve.

We hear quite a bit about what's wrong in the world and see too little action to find effective solutions. While political discussions focus on the extreme left or right, very few seem focused on the 'extreme forward' actions needed to overcome serious national and global challenges.

Many people don't know how to effectively propose ideas and often become frustrated with their organizations' inability to capitalize on their great ideas. This book provides perceptive insights and proactive strategies to improve your ability to successfully innovate and 'lead from the middle' to produce constructive change.

I first wrote about the challenges of leading *from the middle* as an Excellence in Government (EIG) Fellow while serving in the Coast

Guard. EIG Fellows worked on projects to lead people, lead change, and get results for the American public. Many Fellows encountered challenges implementing projects where we didn't control staff, resources, or policy. My sponsor, Rear Admiral Thad Allen (later Commandant serving Presidents Bush and Obama as the federal lead for Hurricane Katrina and the Deepwater Horizon oil spill) wisely informed me, "What you observe, what you learn—how people stall, derail or sidetrack improvement initiatives and changes to the status quo, and then successfully working around those obstacles to keep initiatives on track—will prove to be your most valuable lesson." I captured my experience in a white paper discussing challenges and strategies to exert influence and have impact when you aren't in charge. A year later, the Council for Excellence in Government asked me to conduct "Leading from the Middle" workshops for the EIG Fellows based on my paper.

Later, I practiced what I learned at an enterprise-wide level by chairing the Commandant's newly formed Innovation Council. My job included encouraging people at all levels to voice their ideas, be proactive, and take initiative to improve their part of the organization. We established an Innovation Program that included an annual Expo, awards, scholarships, and a modest fund to pilot test the best ideas. The program started small. The first Innovation Expo was held in 2001 at the Coast Guard Academy but then expanded exponentially, grow-ing seven-fold over the next three years. The Expo eventually attracted twenty-five hundred participants annually including from the Depart-ment of Defense (DOD) and Department of Homeland Security (DHS) agencies. Over twenty-eight nations sent representatives to the Expo to see cutting edge technology and learn the latest operational tactics, logistics systems, and personnel training. Innovation awards inspired people and recognized improvements as diverse as estab-lishing an agency wide information portal and improving helicopter pilot simulation training. Another initiative involved partnering with an academic institution. Over seven hundred Coast Guard personnel earned master's degrees and produced projects valued at over $500 million!

The Coast Guard Innovation Program inspired me to learn more about leading from the middle and strategies to help others lead from wherever they are in their organizations. I conducted academic research that showed in addition to significantly improving organizational performance, innovators also have much higher job satisfaction than their peers. Empowered innovators are more committed and happier in their jobs! Friends and colleagues encouraged me to write about successful strategies used by leaders at all levels to initiate positive change. I hope the stories encourage and inspire you to make things better and the strategies assist you in wisely choosing where and how you can make a difference and be successful. The road isn't easy, but it *is* rewarding!

Geoff Abbott, Captain,
United States Coast Guard, (Retired), DBA

Chapter One

DARE TO LEAD FROM THE MIDDLE

Every great dream begins with a dreamer. Always remember,
you have within you the strength, the patience, and the
passion to reach for the stars to change the world.
~ Harriet Tubman

Conventional wisdom assumes effective leadership comes from executives providing goals, objectives, and directives, which filter down through division directors, managers, and supervisors, and—eventually—to frontline workers. Most organizations use this traditional pyramid structure to execute work and accomplish their mission. The very idea of people leading *from the middle* may seem absurd and possibly irresponsible. And, what exactly do we mean by *leading from the middle* anyway?

Think about a senior leader you respect. The leader likely sets the organization's vision, goals, and objectives with top advisors. However, when executing the plan, top leaders rarely determine and solve problems themselves. Most often, problems are identified and resolved by people at all levels: a clerk realizing critical parts were shipped to the wrong plant, an information technology (IT) specialist providing essential data to key personnel, or the manager realizing she needs to quickly replace a key, recently retired employee. Solution providers are often those closest to the process or customer. They're the ones who

know their system's strengths and weaknesses and the people performing the work.

The concept of *leading from the middle* doesn't just apply to middle
managers, but to anyone, at any level, who influences or initiates constructive change to improve performance, often beyond their formal
level of authority. This can be from the newest staff member suggesting
a better process for training new employees, to the company president
realizing she needs the board of director's support to achieve a competitive advantage.

The key point is we're *all* 'in the middle' when we have an insight to
make a significant improvement, but we're unable to do it by ourselves.
We often need buy-in, support, and the help of others. Often people
with visionary ideas aren't at the top, but are ordinary people close to
the process who realize there's a better way. The following two stories during Hurricane Katrina and the flooding of New Orleans demonstrate ordinary people performing their jobs differently than their
peers using nontraditional methods and achieving dramatic results.

Hurricane Katrina: A Tale of Two Petty Officers

Sometimes during disasters, out of a sense of urgency and necessity
to meet the mission, people develop creative solutions that may not
exactly follow the *rules* or the way things are normally done. Let's see
how two Coast Guard petty officers adapted their jobs to accomplish
the mission during Hurricane Katrina.

Saving Lives in New Orleans

In September 2005, I deployed with several Coast Guard personnel
to assist with the response to Hurricane Katrina, which devastated
New Orleans. I flew to Mobile, Alabama, before being transported by
Coast Guard helicopter to the USS IWO JIMA, a Navy amphibious
assault ship docked at the New Orleans waterfront. While in Mobile,
I asked the Air Station commanding officer about rescuing people
in New Orleans the first few days after the levees were breached. He

said, "Geoff, it was surreal. It was like flying into a sea of fireflies." He then described the view from the helicopter cockpit at night: tens of thousands of flickering pinpoints of light. There was no power, nor any lights because the emergency generators had run out of fuel. There were no cars on the flooded roads, just the pinpoints of what appeared to be wavering lights. As the pilots got closer, they realized they were looking at tens of thousands of people stranded on their balconies, rooftops, and garages, all waving flashlights and waiting to be rescued.

He then told me a story that still gives me chills today. During one rescue operation, the team left their rescue swimmer, the petty officer who helps safely hoist people in the rescue basket, on a residential rooftop while they left to refuel the helicopter. When they returned, the rescue swimmer was visibly upset – enraged, totally frustrated, and grieving. The puzzled pilot asked, "What happened?" The rescue swimmer replied, "Sir, after the helicopter left, I could hear banging and shouting underneath the roof from a family trapped in the attic. Water was already above the second story windows and still rising. I couldn't get to them. I pulled off some shingles but ran into plywood sheathing I couldn't kick through. I'm afraid that family drowned because I didn't have the tools I needed to rescue them. Damn it, sir! I joined the Coast Guard and became a rescue swimmer to save lives, not to lose them!"

After completing several rescues, the helicopter team returned to Mobile past midnight. Before retiring for the night, the rescue swimmer and a couple buddies drove to a local hardware store and bought every fire ax they had in stock. The next morning, the Air Station equipped every helicopter with a fire ax the rescue swimmers could use to hack through rooftops to save people trapped in their attics. Word quickly spread and other Coast Guard Air Stations, Navy, and National Guard units equipped their helicopters with fire axes. This simple equipment addition saved dozens of people trapped in their attics.

Thank goodness for the Coast Guard – not the helicopters, boats, or rescue swimmers, but the procurement specialists!

Two weeks later, at a congressman's meeting about the shortcomings of the federal response to Hurricane Katrina, I ran into a senior civilian from DHS I'd met while deployed in New Orleans. He shook my hand and said, "Thank goodness for the Coast Guard!" I smiled and asked, "Are you referring to helicopter pilots, rescue swimmers, or boat crews?" He shook his head and said, "No, I'm talking about your procurement specialists." A bit surprised, I said, "I haven't heard this story, you have to fill me in."

He observed operations at a Federal Emergency Management Agency (FEMA) logistics center that ordered materials and equipment for the response and recovery from Hurricane Katrina. While most procurement specialists were from FEMA, other agencies contributed personnel to help handle the massive workload. As he observed the process for approving procurement requests from local, state, and federal agency first responders, he noted the FEMA staff had large piles of paper in their in-boxes. He also noticed the Coast Guard petty officer assisting them had a much smaller pile waiting to be processed. He assumed they didn't give the petty officer as many documents due to his inexperience with emergency procurement rules, but this wasn't the case. They gave him just as many documents to process as his peers; he just completed them faster.

My friend spoke with the FEMA staff and the petty officer to learn why they processed documents at different rates. The FEMA procurement specialists reviewed the materials/services requests and compared the requested goods or services to the *authorized* emergency procurement list preapproved by FEMA. If the materials/services weren't on the preapproved list, they denied the request or set it aside for a higher-level review. Problematic procurement requests waited until exceptionally busy officials had time to review them.

The Coast Guard petty officer took a different approach. He reviewed the requests and compared them to the list of *unauthorized* materials and services. Unless the materials/services were on the unauthorized list, or in his judgment were inappropriate, he approved the requests. When asked why he thought he could deviate from FEMA's standard practice he explained, "In the Coast Guard, we're taught to take 'trained initiative' because the actual situation in a massive oil spill or hurricane response is often different than what the manual says." The damage from Hurricane Katrina was unprecedented, and first responders and recovery personnel encountered situations they'd never seen before: alligators swimming in flooded houses, dead cows in trees due to a twenty-plus-foot storm surge, and people trapped in attics. They did their best to come up with solutions, many of which required materials or services not envisioned in FEMA's authorized procurement manual. The petty officer explained, "I'm trusting that the vast majority of first responders are doing their best and order materials and services needed to accomplish their mission. I'll keep alert for possible abuses, but I'm not going to second-guess their procurement request simply because it may be nontraditional and not on the authorized list."

The petty officer intended to keep using this procedure until he was told to stop. But that didn't happen. Instead, other procurement specialists learned how and why he processed documents, and decided they'd process their documents using the same rationale. My DHS friend stated that within a short time, the efficiency of the entire logistics center greatly increased, the backlog of requests was substantially reduced, and the complaints of first responders and recovery personnel about not getting critically needed supplies and equipment significantly decreased.

Leading from the Middle
While these two stories describe different situations, the rescue swimmer involved in life and death operational missions and the procurement specialist in an administrative support role, both petty officers achieved incredible results by making constructive changes to the

way their jobs had been traditionally performed. Clearly, both were motivated by their mission to save lives and provide materials and services legitimately required by first responders as quickly as possible at fair costs. They weren't motivated by self-promotion—rather, they weighed the potential outcome of taking initiative and being proactive versus the consequences of not changing the status quo and accepted "safe" procedures.

Both clearly knew their jobs and assumed risks after assessing what was necessary and appropriate to accomplish their mission. The rescue swimmer and his friends not only bought fire axes with their own funds, without regard to reimbursement, but they introduced a potentially dangerous piece of equipment onto a helicopter prone to significant vibrations and violent motions. They had to determine how to secure the fire ax so it wouldn't come free and strike an occupant or cut a vital hydraulic line threatening the safety of all on board.

Likewise, the procurement specialist assumed the risk someone may attempt an inappropriate procurement that he might not catch. But he also knew he had a limit on his authority to approve procurements (up to twenty-five-hundred dollars). Thus, he weighed the potential for a small number of inappropriate procurements versus the detrimental impact of not providing first responders the equipment and services they needed. He chose to extend trust to those on the front lines to expedite the process and support the time-critical mission to save lives, instead of playing it safe to ensure no bad procurements occurred. He knew he could be at risk from an aggressive auditor, but he could demonstrate that he made the best decisions he could to support the time-critical mission while taking steps to ensure nearly all procurements were legitimate.

So, what motivates individuals to be proactive and take initiative, even when risks are involved? Both were highly motivated to accomplish the mission of saving lives and protecting property, either directly or by enabling first responders. Among the most rewarding factors for both petty officers as they led *from the middle* were 1) making a major contribution to the mission; and 2) having their solutions implemented and incorporated by others, thus multiplying the impact of their contributions.

Why is it important to be proactive and take initiative instead of waiting for management to direct our activities? Often, executives are concerned with political considerations, turf issues, budget constraints, union concerns, and legal issues, which inhibit them from providing timely and clear directions to employees. That doesn't mean we need to sit by in *neutral,* coasting through the day giving sixty to seventy percent of our efforts until management finally provides clear focus and guidance. This would be a disservice to ourselves as well as our organizations. Instead, we can take initiative, regardless of our level in the organization, to improve our workplaces and develop good ideas to influence activities to accomplish our mission. Organizations that understand the power of engaged workers at all levels—and empower them—have a distinct competitive advantage, which means their organization and employees are more capable of achieving their goals.

The term "*unauthorized progress*" focuses on *progress* and moving the organization forward. "*Unauthorized*" shouldn't be misinterpreted as actions that might be frowned upon by management, but rather, it means taking action on the many excellent ideas people have to help achieve goals the organization may not yet recognize, or lags in implementing. *Unauthorized Progress* refers to progress being made, even though the initiative taken hasn't *yet* been fully sanctioned by management. In other words, people don't wait to be told what to do to make improvements or to achieve the mission.

The challenge is to identify great ideas, assess the risks and opportunities, communicate your ideas so they can be improved upon and accepted by others, and successfully implement your ideas while continually learning and refining them to increase their effectiveness and value.

The flowchart on the next page lays out a straightforward process for communicating, evaluating, testing, and implementing your best ideas.

Figure 1.1:   Leading Change from the Middle Flowchart

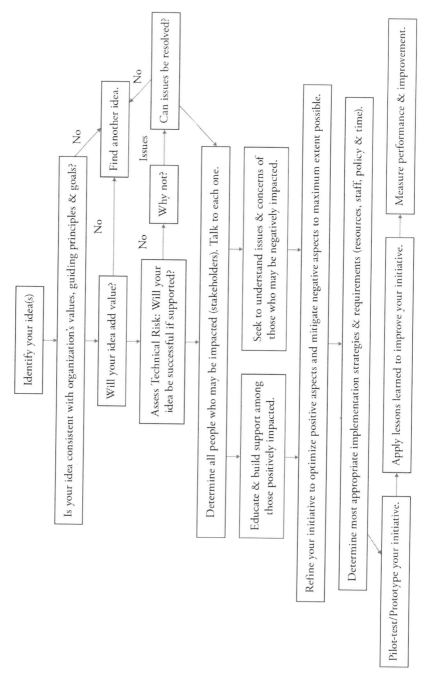

Ordinary People Achieving Extraordinary Results

This book describes stories of ordinary people at all levels, who achieved extraordinary results. These people, and thousands like them, found ways to effectively influence or initiate positive change, and so can you! In addition to the experiences of the Coast Guard rescue swimmer and procurement specialist during Hurricane Katrina you'll meet:

- A lieutenant advocating a professional development program resulting in over seven hundred Coast Guard employees earning master's degrees and producing projects valued at over $500 million
- A government advisor meeting Afghan village elders to improve a controversial military strategy to protect medical convoys in the mountains of Afghanistan
- A visionary Air Force officer suggesting to the Secretary of the Air Force that a wartime capability be shared with FEMA to save lives during domestic disasters
- A Coast Guard civilian challenging a dubious Pentagon policy not allowing DOD dive teams to assist with removal of underwater environmental concerns
- And several others

 Strategies

These are included in every chapter to help you put your ideas into action. All are notated by the icon you see here so you can quickly identify them.

1. *Decide and commit to "Making a Difference."* Focus on one specific area you can influence that's not too broad (e.g., volunteering to help a food bank for the homeless in your community versus trying to solve world hunger). Once your initiative has proven successful, consider how the concept may be expanded to broaden the benefits.

2. *Determine where you'd benefit by increasing your skills, knowledge, and abilities (your competencies).* Three areas proven to be most beneficial for expanding anyone's capacity to lead from the middle include:

   a. **Technical skills:** Specific expertise, experience, and knowledge of the issue/challenge you want to improve

   b. **Business skills:** Business and project management abilities to thoughtfully plan your change initiative, consider what's most valuable to your organization, foresee potential pitfalls and opportunities, and estimate your requirements (resources, policy changes, identify key decision makers)

   c. **Relationship skills:** Even if you have excellent technical and business skills, unless you have exceptional people skills, you'll be limited in your potential to achieve success. Relationship-building and networking skills are critical to clearly communicate your ideas, gain input and feedback, and broaden support

3. *Look for opportunities to expand your knowledge and experience in technical, business, and relationship skills.* Opportunities may include college or professional development courses, cross-training, intern positions, or volunteering in an area of interest.

Summary

I have an almost complete disregard of precedent, and a faith in the possibility of something better. It irritates me to be told how things have always been done. I defy the tyranny of precedent. I go for anything new that might improve the past.
~ Clara Barton

This chapter explained the concept of *leading from the middle*, identified the process to develop and successfully implement great ideas, and demonstrated how ordinary people, using effective strategies, can achieve meaningful and often extraordinary results.

Next *UP*: How you, personally, can become a "Pro-spirator" and make a difference in your organization.

Chapter Two

THE POWER OF EXPERTISE

You cannot hope to build a better world without
improving the individuals. To that end, each of us must
work for our own improvement. ~ *Dr. Marie Curie*

What constructive changes do you want to initiate? Why haven't you acted on those changes? What holds you back? How can you improve your chances for success? This chapter examines the power and influence of individuals and the extraordinary contributions ordinary people make every day. You can too! Each of us has unique experiences and skills that result in specific strengths we can leverage to improve our lives, communities, and organizations. Likewise, there are skills we still need to acquire or enhance to be successful in the future. In this chapter, you'll identify the skills you'll need to succeed in your change efforts; you'll also examine activities you can undertake to enhance your skills in three critical areas: 1) Technical/Operational skills, 2) Business/Project Management skills, and 3) Relationship/Networking skills.

Be a Pro-spirator

This book's short title, *Unauthorized Progress*, may lead you to believe it's for people who conspire to work around management to make progress, despite the bureaucracy. This perception of innovators and risk takers can leave a negative impression with supervisors and managers who also want to achieve progress, but must work within a system of policy, procurement, and personnel constraints. Supervisors and managers don't like being surprised by new initiatives, especially if the surprises negatively impact or have unintended consequences on their other priorities. As a result, some managers, concerned that their carefully crafted plans may be disrupted, don't empower capable employees.

Rather than be a *con*spirator, I encourage you to become a *pro*spirator and develop a reputation for finding solutions and overcoming challenges within existing parameters. The difference is significant in the eyes of leadership, whose support you need to implement any major change initiative. A prospirator works to create positive change for their organization, maintains transparency about their intentions, and makes their immediate supervisor aware of what they're trying to do and why. While obtaining your supervisor's backing for your idea isn't always feasible, prospirators are savvy enough to know that gaining their supervisor's support can help them succeed in several ways:

- Increase trust with your supervisor. Your supervisor is likely to sympathize with what you're trying to accomplish and why and may openly listen to your ideas for how.
- If you have a good relationship with your supervisor, they may act as a coach, guiding you around minefields, making helpful connections, providing timely advice, and opening doors of opportunity.
- Even if they don't agree with your approach, they may decide not to get in your way.

Become an Expert

Each of us has skills, knowledge, and abilities based on our unique life experiences that develop into personal strengths. As we gain experience through education, professional development, research, and work assignments, we gain expertise and may develop a reputation as someone to turn to for advice or to consult with as a subject matter expert. People with credible expertise in areas important to their organizations can often influence or initiate positive action, regardless of their position. The following story illustrates the power of being an expert in an area important to the organization.

Expertise Knows No Rank

I served as executive assistant to a two-star admiral in charge of Coast Guard engineering and communications programs. The admiral attended quarterly meetings at the Pentagon with his Department of Defense peers and their senior staffs to discuss strategic communications and IT issues. Navy admirals, Army, and Air Force generals had their senior staff accompany them, while only a junior lieutenant accompanied the Coast Guard admiral. Although several ranks junior to Navy captains and Army and Air Force colonels, the Coast Guard lieutenant (I'll call him Charlie) had spent many years rising through the enlisted ranks, serving at communications stations around the globe. He was one of a select few enlisted specialists to be chosen for the officer ranks.

Now my admiral was no slouch, in fact many considered him brilliant, as he was the only active duty Coast Guard admiral with a Ph.D. Despite this, he relied heavily on Charlie's advice and expertise for communications policy and technology issues. To say Charlie had a strong influence on the admiral and Coast Guard communications policy would be an understatement.

But Charlie's positive influence extended beyond Coast Guard communications issues. The admiral told me that the colonels and captains attending Pentagon meetings would nearly come unglued when their superiors would talk with the Coast Guard—by far the smallest military service—to ask the "Coasties" about their insights on communications issues. What really galled them was that their senior officers weren't speaking to the Coast Guard admiral most times, but instead were asking Charlie, a low-ranking lieutenant, for his advice on highly complex communications systems. The reason for their interest, in his opinion, was simple. Charlie was one of the most experienced and knowledgeable experts within a highly specialized area of communications of great interest to the DOD. By being a highly regarded, legitimate expert, Charlie was able to influence, not only the Coast Guard, but also national security communications strategy and policy.

"The Places You'll Go" (as an Expert!)

Becoming an expert may take you to new places and allow you to influence events well beyond your traditional role. As an Excellence in Government Fellow, I wrote a white paper on guidelines for leading from the middle and asked some Coast Guard colleagues and senior leaders for feedback. One admiral was particularly intrigued by the strategy of *becoming an expert* and told me that he'd done that many times in his career.

As a young officer, he investigated incidents involving whitewater rafting casualties on the Colorado River. After meeting experts, conducting stability calculations, and experiencing the Colorado River himself on whitewater rafting expeditions, he became a technical expert on the many reasons rafts capsized, which endangered their occupants. Due to his expertise, he was asked to testify before Congress about increasing whitewater rafting safety, normally a responsibility conducted by admirals.

Later in his career, as a new admiral, he became the agency's chief information officer (CIO). His major challenge: to make sure the Coast Guard and global maritime interests were well prepared for "Y2K"—the concern that critical computer program subroutines would not function, or worse, go haywire, on New Years' morning as the millennium changed from 1999 to 2000. Fears about Y2K impacted the entire globe and the admiral was responsible for minimizing its impact, not just on Coast Guard operations, but on the global maritime industry as well. Fortunately, he had a talented and capable staff and, as the months ticked off toward January 1, 2000, he became expert at understanding how the potential consequences of a "Y2K bug" could impact ship and Global Positioning navigation systems (GPS) and oversaw the development of effective mitigation strategies. Due to his expertise, the White House asked him to speak at the Group of Eight (G8) Economic Conference. He also became the first Coast Guard officer ever to address the United Nations General Assembly, not once, but twice, on the risks of Y2K incidents and mitigation strategies to ensure safe and efficient maritime commerce.

It's About "Attitude" Not "Altitude"

Leading from the middle is about your attitude toward contributing to your organization, not how high up the organizational hierarchy you are. Charlie was nowhere near the top of the military officer ranks, yet he had a large influence on Coast Guard and DOD communications technology strategy. He effectively served as an advisor to the top brass because of his subject matter expertise in areas of critical importance to his organization.

The best managers don't focus on how to "fix" their people and deal with shortcomings. Rather, they play to the strengths of their people and build teams where their strengths complement each other and cover any individual's shortcomings. They've learned people are much more energized and engaged when using their strengths to contribute to their team or organization.

What about you? Have you considered your collective knowledge, experiences, skills, and the unique strengths you have? Once you understand these, you can establish your current strengths baseline and determine which ones to expand upon to become the "go-to person" in your organization.

Who Are the Agents of Change? Where Do They Come From?

Who exactly are the people willing and often compelled to influence and initiate positive change? Who are the ones not waiting to be told what to do, but leading from the middle? What do they have in common? Educational background? Similar job functions? Age range or generation? What motivates them to take on additional work and risks? Why do they do it, and what rewards are truly meaningful for them? Are they happier and more content in their work, or more frustrated due to the perceived snail's pace of progress in their organizations?

I explored these questions to better understand why people became change agents and how to encourage them to improve organizational performance. I developed a survey and received responses from one hundred seventy Coast Guard innovators. Based on my experience, I wasn't surprised to find Coast Guard innovators came from a variety of backgrounds. Innovators ranged from their twenties to their sixties; worked at operational commands, training and support units; and had specialties as diverse as helicopter pilots, professional mariners, IT specialists, budget analysts, and trainers. They came from all levels, from junior petty officers to seasoned senior officers, new and veteran civilian employees, reservists, and even Coast Guard auxiliarists (volunteers who assist with boating safety and search and rescue).

Motivation: Coast Guard innovators' responses concerning their motivation, empowerment, job satisfaction and meaningful rewards were intriguing. While bonuses and monetary awards are a primary means of recognition for excellent work in the private sector, cash awards ranked eighth among innovators' meaningful awards. Innovators are motivated and "jazzed" by successfully improving a process or making a positive change in the organization and by being recognized for their contribution in front of their peers. The most frequent responses concerning innovators' characteristics, motivation, and meaningful rewards are:

"What are Innovators' most common characteristics?"

1. High motivation
2. Open to new ideas and creative
3. Not afraid of taking risks and failing

"What motivates you?"

1. Personal drive
2. Desire to improve and constructively change the organization
3. Improve organizational efficiency

"What rewards are most meaningful to you?"

1. Recognition (formal or informal)
2. Implementation of my idea/concept
3. Improved organizational performance

Empowerment/Job Satisfaction: The most intriguing finding was the relationship between empowerment and job satisfaction. I had long suspected people who felt empowered and often worked longer hours to improve their workplace were happier and more committed to their organizations. When I reviewed the results, I was stunned. The Coast Guard innovator responses averaged *significantly* higher, in both empowerment and job satisfaction, than Coast Guard colleagues, DHS colleagues, and government employees overall.

In addition, innovators' responses overwhelmingly supported a strong, positive relationship between being empowered and taking initiative to their job satisfaction and commitment to the organization.

*   "Highly motivated employees who are encouraged to take initiative and risks to improve the organization have increased job satisfaction." Result: 90.6% positive response
*   "Highly motivated employees who are encouraged to take initiative and risks to improve the organization have a higher commitment to the organization." Result: 92.0% positive response

This research indicates that in organizations with supportive cultures, anyone with personal drive and motivation can be a change agent and initiate or influence positive change, regardless of their age, position, specialty, or functional area.

 Strategies

1. **Identify your strengths.** We're all good at some things, even if we have limited experience. You may have good analytic skills; athletic abilities; creative and artistic talents; great relationship, compassion, and empathy skills, or you may be great at video games and IT. With your unique life experiences—family upbringing, high school activities, college, athletics, clubs, your first job—you gain skills and talents which determine your individual strengths. Some strengths you're aware of, while others may be more subtle or even hidden. You can identify your strengths through personal reflection, grades, or performance evaluations, as well as asking family members, friends, and coworkers what they believe your strengths are.

2. **Identify where you need to improve to make an impact.** Consider where you need to improve in your technical competencies, business and project management skills, and relationship and networking skills. In my experience observing and assisting hundreds of Coast Guard innovators, these three areas, technical competence, business/management skills, and people/relationship skills are areas you can most directly and positively improve with thoughtful planning and initiative.

3. **Identify specific actions to improve your expertise.** Once you've identified specific skills, experience, or strengths you need to acquire or enhance, determine what constructive actions you can take to increase your competencies in these key areas.

4. **Develop and execute a plan to improve your expertise in areas important to your organization!** After determining

viable actions to improve your expertise, develop a game plan. Consider your short- and long-term goals, the real-world constraints on your time and resources, and the impacts both will have on your professional and personal life. Think strategically about which actions would be most beneficial and have the highest return on your investment. Consider if actions should be done in a specific order. For instance, you may want to do online research on a technical topic prior to speaking with a subject matter expert. You can't do everything at once, so you need to prioritize activities to continually make progress without burning out.

Summary

Without continual growth and progress, such words as improvement, achievement, and success have no meaning. ~ Benjamin Franklin

This chapter focused on understanding your unique skills, experiences, and strengths; identifying areas you may want to enhance; and developing a plan to take specific actions to expand your expertise. But nothing will change for you personally until you commit to a goal and action plan to enhance your knowledge, experience, and skills, and establish your credibility with decision makers. Know your strengths, identify areas to build upon, and determine a strategy and specific actions to increase your expertise. What are you waiting for? Who knows where this exciting path will take you? The Pentagon, a G8 Economic Summit overseas, or even the United Nations! It's time to get started, *now!*

Next *UP*: Determine which critical issues to work on to make an impact. Where do great ideas come from?

Chapter Three

THINK STRATEGICALLY; DRIVE RESULTS

When it is obvious that the goals cannot be reached,
don't adjust the goals, adjust the action steps.
~ Confucius

You know things need to get better in your organization, and you may have already identified one or two areas you'd like to improve to really make a difference. How do you start? How do you determine where to focus your energy? Often the choices are obvious: superiors may direct you to address a certain problem or challenge. Key stakeholders, major customers, or those already working on the process being improved can be a source of good ideas. Sometimes, the direction to pursue isn't so obvious and all you know is the organization needs to improve in a specific area. In these cases, using the power of imagination can be helpful to ask thought-provoking questions such as, "What if . . .?" "Why don't we . . .?" and "How else might we achieve our goal more effectively or efficiently?"

In cases where the path forward isn't clear or there may be several viable directions and potential solutions, applying tools consultants use to focus clients on their most urgent and pressing issues may help. One tool to identify potential trouble areas or opportunities is a Strengths, Weaknesses, Opportunities, Threats (SWOT) Analysis. In a SWOT analysis, you ask the following questions about an area you plan to improve.

- What are the organization's <u>Strengths</u> and <u>Weaknesses</u> in this area?
- What are the <u>Opportunities</u> for and the <u>Threats</u> to our organization in dealing with this issue?

A well-facilitated SWOT analysis with knowledgeable staff can quickly generate several excellent ideas.

However, having several excellent ideas raises another issue. How do you decide which to work on first? It's often useful to employ an "Importance versus Urgency" matrix to show both the degree of importance and level of urgency for each issue.

Identifying Critical Challenges/Opportunities

The SWOT analysis method, developed by Albert Humphrey of the Stanford Research Institute (now SRI) in the 1970s, involves identifying internal and external factors that are favorable or unfavorable to achieving a specific organizational objective.

- **Strengths:** Organization or project characteristics that provide an advantage
- **Weaknesses:** Organization or project characteristics that are disadvantageous
- **Opportunities:** Elements that could benefit the initiative or organization
- **Threats:** Elements that could harm the initiative or organization

To perform a SWOT analysis, you must determine the strengths, weaknesses, opportunities, and threats regarding your objective. The next step is to identify specific achievable solution paths knowing the risks and benefits of various approaches.

Table 3.1:   SWOT Analysis Template

SWOT	Helpful	Harmful
Internal	Strengths	Weaknesses
External	Opportunities	Threats

One useful tool for comparing and prioritizing issues is the "Importance versus Urgency Matrix." Integrating these often-competing components in a matrix has been credited to both President Eisenhower and Dr. Stephen Covey. Eisenhower used the importance/urgency concept to prioritize his tasks. Dr. Covey made the concept known more broadly in his book, *The Seven Habits of Highly Effective People*. This technique involves a two-by-two matrix with an issue's importance on one axis and its urgency on the other as shown in Table 3.2.

Urgency and Importance are defined in the matrix as:

Urgency: issues demanding immediate or short-term attention

Importance: initiatives contributing to achieving long-term organizational goals, values, or the mission

Using the issues you developed during your SWOT analysis, plot each in the matrix for comparison purposes. Each issue's location in the matrix indicates its priority and the potential impact of a successful solution.

Table 3.2: Importance Versus Urgency Matrix

	High Urgency	Low Urgency
High Importance	High Importance and Urgency issues should be addressed first	High Importance-Low Urgency issues are often deferred due to a focus on High Urgency issues
Low Importance	Organizations often work on High Urgency issues that aren't important	Low Importance and Low Urgency issues should be dropped

Most organizations recognize high importance and high urgency issues (top left quadrant) they face and make those a top priority. They also recognize low importance and low urgency issues (bottom right quadrant) and don't waste time on them. However, many organizations spend valuable time on high urgency, but low importance matters, and often defer high importance but low urgency issues. Focusing your efforts on finding solutions to the issues of the greatest importance to your organization (top two quadrants) will have the greatest impact.

Maine Lighthouses

From 1995 to 1998, I commanded a Civil Engineering Unit at Providence, Rhode Island responsible for supporting Coast Guard facilities—small boat stations, air stations, support centers, major bases, and lighthouses—from mid-New Jersey to Maine. In addition to engineering design and construction services, we conducted master planning, environmental, and real property functions.

Maintaining sixty historic Maine lighthouses became one of our greatest challenges. Major renovations of historic lighthouses typically cost $250,000 to $400,000 each due to National Historic Preservation Act requirements, environmental regulations, remote locations, and a short construction season. With a constrained construction budget dedicated for operational support facilities (e.g., runways, hangars, docks, piers, communications, and command centers) and personnel support (family housing, barracks, and food services), limited funds existed for unmanned, remote historic structures. Lighthouse maintenance costs escalated rapidly, and we fell further and further behind maintaining these historic structures that played an essential role in our nation's maritime development.

Ted, a mid-grade civilian, led our real property activities. Ted considered federal property and facilities as assets that could be leveraged to reduce operational and support costs. He had an entrepreneurial spirit and frequently identified innovative ideas to leverage the value of our real property assets. Ted knew the significant impact that lighthouse renovations had on our construction budget. He also understood the frustration over our inability to maintain them to our standards due to limited resources.

So *how* are good ideas originated? To solve the lighthouse maintenance challenge, the solution began with an unconstrained thinker knowledgeable about the problem and expert in a helpful area – real property law and regulations.

A representative of a nonprofit group asked to meet Ted at a local restaurant in Maine to discuss Coast Guard lighthouses. His organization wanted to acquire a local lighthouse for community educational purposes. Ted described the lengthy process for acquiring lighthouses through the General Services Administration (GSA). He explained that an available lighthouse would be offered first to federal, state, and local agencies. If those agencies weren't interested, the lighthouse could then be offered for purchase by local nonprofit organizations. Ted also mentioned that lighthouses had been transferred by congressional action in some cases.

Because Ted understood real property law and regulations, he was in a perfect position to see an opportunity that would benefit many. He asked, "Why are you only interested in one lighthouse, when there are two in the local area?" The representative indicated he'd have to discuss a larger acquisition with his board of directors. Ted pressed further. "But why just two lighthouses? Why not five or ten or twenty?" The representative's eyes opened wide and he said his organization could never support that many lighthouses. However, this comment didn't stop Ted. "I researched your organization and know the good work it's done in Maine. You should be proud of being a good role model for nonprofit organizations contributing to their communities. Why not create a process for other outstanding nonprofit organizations to have the same opportunity you seek?" Ted wasn't sure he'd gotten through to the representative as they said their goodbyes. He didn't think he'd hear from him again.

But the next Monday, Ted received a call from the representative who asked, "If someone introduced legislation transferring lighthouses to the Island Institute, what conditions would the Coast Guard need to service the lights and fog signals?" This question began a lengthy negotiation that resulted in a process to transfer ownership of up to thirty-six lighthouses to local communities or nonprofit organizations that met specific environmental and historic restoration guidelines, developed an effective fundraising strategy, and allowed Coast Guard access to lighthouse equipment.

U.S. Senator George Mitchell (D-Maine) introduced a congressional amendment to transfer lighthouses to well-qualified organizations selected by a commission chosen by Maine's governor. Unfortunately, the president vetoed the bill for reasons unrelated to lighthouses. U.S. Senator Olympia Snowe (R-Maine) reintroduced the amendment the following year and it passed. After reviewing numerous proposals from organizations interested in the thirty-six available lighthouses, the governor's commission selected twenty-eight organizations it believed were best qualified to meet the strict historic restoration and environmental requirements and raise enough funds to meet the financial obligations necessary to maintain the lighthouses.

Ted realized his vision after a lot of networking, negotiations, and contributions by many parties. Not only did both Maine senators and local politicians attend the ceremony to transfer the lighthouses, but also the Senate Appropriations Committee chairman and the Coast Guard Commandant who saw this as a win-win for Maine, the Coast Guard, and federal taxpayers.

So where might great ideas come from? To preserve Maine lighthouses, the idea came from a visionary mid-grade employee with passion and valuable expertise who partnered with an open-minded and progressive external stakeholder to achieve an extraordinary outcome. And it all started with a conversation in a pub over a beer.

Help for Afghanistan

After retiring from the Coast Guard, I worked at a nonprofit think tank created by Congress to provide independent and objective research and analysis for DHS agencies. I met many interesting people in this role, but none more interesting than a gentleman I met for two hours in a tent at a joint DOD/DHS disaster response demonstration. I'll simply call him "Dan." Dan was a man of many talents. By formal training, he knew how the human brain worked and processed information, and he was a key founder of an organization working with paralyzed quadriplegic children. Part of their therapy included teaching them to play video games by blinking their eyes. Dan said, "The kids think they're playing games; their doctors think it's therapy. Perhaps they're both right!"

In another capacity, Dan served as an advisor to government and military officials to assist with early U.S. efforts to stabilize Afghanistan. Dan stated his philosophy this way: "I'm not into destroying the bad guys nearly as much as I believe in saving the good guys." He also strongly believed in what he called the "Mom Test." That is, "Would Mom be proud of my actions, even if they don't necessarily comply one hundred percent with regulations and tradition?"

The U.S. was interested in assisting Afghanistan with building infrastructure essential to its economy, education, energy, and transportation systems and supporting its civil authorities. Dan's job was to develop effective strategies to provide U.S. support to the civilian Afghan government. Dan met a senior Afghan official and asked what nonmilitary activity would make the most significant positive contribution to his nation. The official thought a moment and responded that digitized maps of his entire country would be extraordinarily helpful for developing Geographic Information System (GIS) maps essential for building critical infrastructure for transportation, energy, communications, medical, and education systems. GIS maps would give the government the ability to integrate key systems to provide essential services to the Afghan people.

Two weeks later, digitized maps for the entire Afghanistan geography mysteriously arrived. It was unlikely that permission to create them had been acquired through formal bureaucratic channels because that would have taken months. The Afghan government was able to use these maps to improve the nation's infrastructure on a much faster timeline than expected. Sometimes great ideas come from simply asking the primary beneficiary what they really need and is most important to them. The solutions may already exist within your organization and be known by an effective leader who knows how to cut through the bureaucracy to create timely positive action!

Strategic Thinking and Solution Development

Both stories illustrate examples of people at different levels (a mid-grade federal employee and a high-ranking government official) thinking strategically about potential solutions when approached with an opportunity. When asked about transferring a single lighthouse, Ted thought bigger: Why just one? Why not five or ten or twenty? In the end, twenty-eight lighthouses were transferred to local communities and nonprofit organizations, reducing federal taxpayer expense, and providing a boost to tourism along Maine's rocky coast.

When asked what nonmilitary assistance would be most valuable to his nation, the senior Afghan official didn't think in terms of the conflict raging across the countryside but thought far into the future to what would most help the Afghan people. He didn't think of a single facility such as a dam to provide hydroelectric power, or industry such as the energy sector, but instead thought of creating an information backbone needed to improve all critical infrastructure systems in Afghanistan.

How did Ted and the Afghan official develop the insight that led to visionary solutions? Both were familiar with the strengths and weaknesses of their organizations and the opportunities and threats of their situations. Their knowledge allowed them to assess the risks and benefits of potential solutions and suggest appropriate courses of action. Both took "the long view" when considering what was truly important and valuable. This type of strategic, long-term thinking can result in great benefits to your organization as you work to resolve immediate issues while preparing to successfully deal with future challenges and opportunities.

 Strategies

Use the following strategies to identify and focus on your organization's most important and urgent issues. Once you identify the "critical few" issues, develop potential solutions.

1. **Identify a general opportunity or problem area to explore**: Find one that truly matters and where you can make a difference.

2. **Conduct a SWOT analysis for your opportunity or problem area:** Determine key issues for improvement opportunities.

3. **Prioritize issues for improvement:** Use an Importance versus Urgency matrix to determine which issues to investigate further.

4. **Select your top improvement opportunity:** Develop several preliminary solution concepts.

Summary

> *The secret to getting ahead is getting started.*
> *~ Mark Twain*

This chapter provides a method for identifying the most valuable and urgent issues to work on within your organization using a SWOT analysis. It further provides a process to prioritize these issues for potential exploration using an Importance versus Urgency Matrix. Finally, two examples help to illustrate how strategic approaches to problems can create excellent (and often not obvious) ideas.

Next *UP*: How to influence decision makers to positively receive your solution concepts.

Chapter Four

WICKED PROBLEMS AND OPPORTUNITIES

Thinking is easy, acting is difficult, and to put one's thoughts into action is the most difficult thing in the world. ~ Johann Wolfgang von Goethe

Okay, you're making progress! By now, you know the general area you want to help your organization improve in, you've done a SWOT analysis and discovered the major issues you want to focus on, and you've prioritized those by determining which issues are both important and urgent. You've selected your top issues for further investigation and decided which ones you want to explore first. You might have even conducted a brainstorming session to identify a few ideas to pursue.

But how do you know if your ideas are really any good? How will you not only convince decision makers your approach is sound, but communicate it in a way that resonates with them and gains their support? How do you build a strong and positive case for your initiative to gain preliminary support for a pilot test or prototype development? The answer lies in knowing the major factors decision makers consider when evaluating initiatives.

Deepwater Horizon Drilling Platform Disaster

At 9:45 p.m. CDT on April 20, 2010, gas, oil, and concrete exploded up the wellbore of the Deepwater Horizon oil platform forty-eight miles offshore from Louisiana in the Gulf of Mexico. Tragically, the explosion and platform fire killed eleven workers, injured seventeen, and resulted in one of the largest manmade oil spills in history. Vast amounts of oil spewed from well damage at the ocean floor, a mile below the sea's surface.

One week after the explosion, the spill was one hundred miles across and only twenty miles from the Louisiana coast. Despite the oil industry's and government's best efforts, the spill continued, largely unabated, for four months with over 50,000 barrels of oil per day flowing into the Gulf of Mexico. Five months later, on September 19, British Petroleum, the company responsible, finally declared the well completely and permanently sealed. In total, the Flow Rate Technical Group estimated 4.9 million barrels (205 million U.S. gallons) of oil poured into the sea, washed ashore on pristine beaches and environmentally fragile wetlands from Louisiana to Florida, and closed vast areas of the Gulf to the seafood industry.

Initially, oil industry experts developed and tried several ideas, but all efforts to stop the oil flow failed. British Petroleum established a suggestion program to collect ideas from scientists, engineers, and even private citizens from around the world. President Obama appointed my former boss, retiring Admiral Thad Allen, to be the Principal Federal Official (PFO) for the Deepwater Horizon spill and cleanup. This assignment came on the heels of his completion of a highly successful assignment as Coast Guard Commandant. Admiral Allen tasked the Coast Guard's Research and Development Center with reaching out to the global scientific and engineering community for effective solutions to stop the oil pouring from the seafloor. Environmental groups also participated by setting up blogs where suggestions could be left. Evaluating the hundreds upon hundreds of proposed ideas was an immense challenge, mainly in determining which, if any, might be effectively implemented within a very short timeframe.

Selecting the Best of the Best

While I chaired the Commandant's Innovation Council, we decided to reward fruitful innovation efforts by establishing an annual awards program to recognize creative people, leading from the middle to improve their Coast Guard in Operations & Readiness, Science & Technology, Training & Support, and Management. The Commandant presented the awards at the annual Innovation Expo and sent a message to the entire Coast Guard letting everyone know which of their peers won Innovation Awards.

The first two years, the Innovation Council easily determined recipients for the new awards. However, as word spread, more and more commands nominated their most creative and successful innovators. The Innovation Council found itself sifting through sixty to eighty award applications annually. This raised an interesting dilemma for the Innovation Council, which had a small innovation venture capital fund to invest in the "best of the best" ideas to see if they could be applied more broadly to improve organizational performance.

The varied innovations spread across multiple operational mission and support areas. One year, a civilian, age sixty-plus, who was working at Coast Guard headquarters in the medical support field received an innovation award. During the early years of support for DOD in Kuwait and Iraq, he noted most Coast Guard reservists attached to deploying Port Security Units were from the midwestern United States and had difficulty getting proper physicals for the extreme demands of serving in the Mideast. Several reservists suffered medical incidents and had to be evacuated due to medical conditions that should have been detected by a physical prior to leaving the States.

This civilian was also a member of the Coast Guard Auxiliary, a volunteer organization that supports Coast Guard operations. He knew Auxiliary members with boats who assisted Coast Guard units with flotillas and boating parades, and those with aircraft who assisted the Coast Guard with search and rescue operations. He thought,

"Wouldn't it be great if we had an Auxiliary medical corps to provide exams for Coast Guard personnel deploying overseas?" Then he made it happen! He created a medical corps comprised of four hundred volunteer doctors, nurses, and dentists across the country who provided no-cost medical exams for deploying personnel. The value of this initiative was estimated to be $100,000 the first year alone!

When Terror Strikes

As commanding officer of the Coast Guard's Research and Development Center when terrorists attacked the World Trade Center and the Pentagon on September 11, 2001, our team worked aggressively with operational units to enhance security and eliminate vulnerabilities from U.S. waterways and ports. We received hundreds of suggestions, including ideas from Mexico and China. We had to use limited R&D funds effectively to support Coast Guard operations. Through extensive discussion with key stakeholders and decision makers, we filtered through dozens of ideas and concepts, and then eventually determined five to ten security improvement technologies to pilot test at two ports: San Francisco and Miami. These technologies included concepts such as "blue-force tracking," "tripwire technology," and inter-agency tactical communications, which are now implemented broadly.

Wicked Problems and Opportunities

The 9/11 terrorist attacks, Deepwater Horizon disaster, and Hurricane Katrina response are all situations the Coast Guard has dealt with that many call "wicked problems." These are problems that are nearly impossible to solve due to incomplete or contradictory information, the diversity and number of people and organizations involved, huge costs and human resources needed, and high degree of complexity as these massive problems interconnect with other multifaceted major issues.

But just as these wicked problems represent massive challenges, proactive and empowered bright minds can create what I call "wicked opportunities" or solutions. Such a wicked solution occurred on a college campus after a student questioned why his university cafeteria threw out leftover food nightly. His question led him to start a movement that provided leftover food for the homeless at food banks. Fourteen colleges across the nation joined! Stories of ordinary, proactive people creating wicked opportunities to achieve extraordinary results are revealed in future chapters.

Six Primary Criteria Used to Evaluate Ideas

In each of these situations, Deepwater Horizon, 9/11, and the Innovation Awards, decision makers needed a process to evaluate myriad ideas to address a significant challenge. In my thirty years of active duty working with innovators, research and development solutions, EIG Fellows, and master's students' results projects, I've observed decision makers consistently consider six factors when asked to support solution concepts. Executives want to know that the change agent thoroughly considered both the potential benefits and possible consequences of their proposed solution concept. Executives determine their level of support for the concept by asking key questions and carefully listening to the change agent's responses. These key factors are:

- Relevance
- Value
- Risk
- Supportability
- Downside
- Resource Requirements/Costs

As a change agent, it may seem counterintuitive, but your biggest challenge early on isn't to get decision makers to say "Yes" to your initiative, but rather to do everything you can to keep any single one of them from saying "No." It can take quite a while to develop support and get key players to agree to implement an initiative, but it only takes one decision maker to quickly kill an idea. To overcome this obstacle, you must identify who might be in a position to stop your initiative and for what reasons. Typically, the reasons fall into the following six categories.

Relevance: Is the idea aligned with organizational goals? Is it consistent with your organization's values and guiding principles? Does it address an issue important to your organization or immediate workplace? If decision makers don't see the relevance of your ideas, they won't support your initiative in favor of other ideas more relevant to the organization's goals.

Value: Will the benefits of your solution significantly outweigh the costs? Will the anticipated tangible and intangible benefits exceed the opportunity costs of investing the same resources in another initiative? What makes your initiative stand out, and why should your organization implement your idea over other good ideas it could invest in?

Risk: Will the idea be successful? Will it really work? If not, why not? Play devil's advocate. Identify reasons the concept could fail, then eliminate them, or develop workarounds. Be critical when evaluating and identifying vulnerabilities in your idea. Then, fill the gaps so that your idea will succeed. Mitigate any significant issues to reduce potential consequences, if possible.

Supportability: Do all key stakeholders support your initiative? If not, what are the reasons they don't support it? Can you change their perspective by addressing their concerns? Decision makers consider who's likely to support this initiative and who may fight the change. Legitimate concerns raised by a senior decision maker can quickly kill an idea. Strong support from an influential stakeholder can help build a critical mass of support among key leaders. Do what you can to build support for your concept and eliminate or mitigate negative aspects.

Downside: What are the negative impacts or consequences of your initiative? These are different from the risks of failure. My son, Nick, was striving for Boy Scouting's highest rank, Eagle, which required he complete an extensive project. His first proposal involved building a fence around a dumpster in a church parking lot. It was a good project concept, but it had a downside. The project would eliminate three parking spots next to the dumpster. The Board of Trustees turned down the project because church parking was essential, and they thought the project's benefits didn't outweigh the negative aspects. Nick found another project and earned his Eagle rank. He also learned a valuable lesson about how leaders make decisions.

Resource Requirements/Costs: What resources are required to implement your initiative? Where will they come from? Can you reduce resource requirements without negatively impacting the initiative? Staff time and resources can be difficult to obtain, and the more resources required for your initiative, the more challenging it will be to gain approval. Few organizations have unused resources which means resources required for your initiative must come at the expense of other work/efforts, meaning a decision would have to be made to reduce or stop doing something previously approved. This can be an uphill battle and one you're likely to lose as managers, competing for scarce resources, may actively work against your change proposal unless they see a benefit. This can work to your advantage if your initiative improves efficiency and frees up resources or provides a badly needed capability that doesn't exist currently.

Another option is to look for resources outside of your traditional process or organization. When improving the Coast Guard's Quality Program by educating personnel about best management practices, one of the most effective methods involved encouraging interested personnel to complete a twelve-month master's program in quality systems management. This experiential learning program required students to create a process improvement project that produced a positive return on investment for the organization, including tuition cost, or the students didn't graduate! The tuition cost more than most employees could afford, which posed a significant challenge. We successfully tied the master's program into the Coast Guard's tuition assistance program and offered $2,000 Innovation Scholarships. The Coast Guard's Quality Program significantly improved by tapping into resources available through its tuition assistance and innovation programs. The investment paid off. By 2010, over seven hundred personnel had earned master's degrees while developing process improvement projects valued at $500 million!

Understanding the Strengths and Weaknesses of an Improvement Initiative

How can you identify the strengths and weaknesses of your solution to determine which areas to improve prior to submitting a proposal to decision makers? Read the following statements, either by yourself or with a few colleagues who understand your change initiative, and then score them one to five as indicated.

   Scoring:

1. *Strongly Disagree*
2. *Disagree*
3. *Neutral*
4. *Agree*
5. *Strongly Agree*

Success Criteria Statements:

- **Relevance:** This initiative is closely aligned with, contributes to, or achieves organizational goals.
- **Value:** This initiative, if implemented successfully, will have a high return on investment.

- **Risk:** This initiative has a high probability of technical success and isn't overly complex.

- **Support:** This initiative is likely to gain broad support among stakeholders and leaders.

- **Downside:** This initiative has relatively minor negative aspects that can be largely mitigated.

- **Resources:** This initiative can be implemented and sustained through available funding/staffing resources.

Virtually no initiative will receive all top scores. Think about your idea from many perspectives. Why might a decision maker hesitate to support your initiative? Statements receiving lower scores may highlight vulnerabilities and provide you with opportunities for improving your solution concept.

 Strategies

1. **Understand and know how to apply the six success criteria.** Decision makers use these to evaluate new initiatives for potential success.

2. **Evaluate and compare your top solution concepts.** Use the success criteria to compare your top solution concepts. Be brutally honest in your evaluation of the pros and cons of your solution concepts for each success criteria. Take a challenging, devil's advocate approach to evaluating your concepts and identify areas to improve to receive the support of key decision makers. Identify anything that would negatively impact your chances of gaining support. If you can't overcome these, consider another solution concept.

3. **Select the most promising concept and improve it.** Identify which criteria can be improved upon. Consider how to broaden

opportunities, increase benefits, reduce any downsides, and lessen risks. Determine what's important to key stakeholders and what may concern them. Build upon your initial concept to make it defendable and bulletproof from naysayers.

Summary

> *Opportunity does not waste time with those who are unprepared. ~ Idowu Koyenikan*

Chapter Four explored how to assess the potential success of your preliminary change concept. We discussed six success criteria decision makers use to determine their support for new initiatives and learned how to score and assess your concept's strengths and weaknesses. Try using this process on a change initiative or process improvement you've been thinking about. It's easy, and once you try it, you'll find how useful this process can be to improve your ideas and gain support from decision makers.

Next UP: How to further develop, evolve, and improve your chosen solution concept.

Chapter Five

FINDING GREAT SOLUTIONS

Good management is the art of making problems so
interesting and their solutions so constructive that
everyone wants to get to work and deal with them.
~ Paul Hawken

You're making progress! You've assessed your concept using the six primary criteria decision makers use to determine their support for a change initiative. You've identified strengths and vulnerabilities and have some ideas as to where to focus your efforts to further refine your concept. Now it's time to reach out to other key players to get their reactions to your idea. In this phase, you will uncover any issues key players have with your concept and expose additional concerns or suggestions they may have.

When considering the support that you need, think broadly. Don't stop at decision makers, implementers, and stakeholders, but also include those key staff who influence these players, as well as advisors and critical support staff (IT, resource/budget, human resources). One of the most important lessons I learned as a new staff member at Coast Guard headquarters was from a senior civilian who told me, "Never circulate a decision memo for signature until you've already won the war. . ." He explained, ". . . before you circulate paper requiring a decision by executives, make sure you've already talked to key staff members in all impacted offices, mitigated their concerns, and gained their support." Heed his advice because you don't want your executive to ask, "Are there any issues still to be addressed or any reasons I shouldn't approve this initiative right now?" If there are still issues to be resolved, you can bet your request won't be signed. In fact, it may be rejected without giving you a second chance to fix the issues that still need to be addressed. Bottom line: Do your homework before submitting the paperwork!

Identify the key players you should talk to about your initiative. Develop a concise explanation of the challenge you plan to overcome and your solution concept. Then discuss it with them. Once you explain your challenge and proposed solution to critical players, the key is to *actively listen* to their comments, issues, and suggestions. Be objective, don't get defensive, and don't minimize their issues or concerns. Show respect by carefully listening to them because they will raise issues you were unaware of and suggest effective solutions you would never think of. Don't forget to ask if they have any ideas to make your plan more effective or efficient, or if there is anyone else they recommend you speak to.

Saving Lives: Protecting Medical Convoys in the Mountains of Afghanistan

In Chapter Three, I introduced Dan, an advisor to Afghan and U.S. government forces in Afghanistan whom I met at a joint DOD/DHS disaster response demonstration. During his time in-country, Dan observed many challenges faced by U.S. and Afghan forces and civil authorities to stabilize the countryside and make it safer for the Afghan people and their allies. One story he told involved non-governmental organizations (NGO) such as the International Red Cross and Red Crescent which provided critical medical supplies to women and children in remote villages. Taliban fighters kept ambushing NGO truck convoys in a narrow mountain pass, killing and wounding NGO workers, destroying vehicles, and stealing valuable medical supplies.

U.S. and Afghan forces strategized on how to minimize this threat. They developed a plan to move the road, so it avoided the mountain pass. The *downside* of the plan was that the option chosen required building the road through an ancient village cemetery filled with the graves of ancestors and respected village leaders that were centuries old.

When Dan heard this plan, he immediately recognized the risk of proceeding. If military forces built the new road through the burial grounds of this historic religious site, it could cause anger and resentment among the villagers, which could enable the Taliban to gain more sympathizers and recruits.

Dan met with military leaders and requested a forty-eight-hour delay before implementing the plan so he could discuss possible options with village leaders. They granted his request, but they doubted it would have any impact on their plan. Dan met with the village elders and showed them the mountain road the convoys took to the village and the narrow mountain pass where the attacks took place. He then explained the military's plan to move the road so trucks would avoid the dangerous pass. He also explained that this route would go through the burial ground of their ancestors, which posed a serious tribal and religious issue. He asked for their wisdom, guidance, and suggestions as to the best way to safely deliver the medicines that were so essential for the village without defiling their traditions and beliefs. The elders thanked Dan for coming to them and asked him to return in two days when they would let him know their advice.

When Dan returned, he couldn't believe what he saw. As he slowly drove by the burial ground, he saw old men and boys with pickaxes and shovels carefully digging up their ancestors' remains to relocate them to a new site.

When Dan met the elders, they gave their blessing for the military to construct the new road. They found a solution that allowed the safe delivery of essential medical supplies to the local population, while avoiding a potential violation of their faith and tribal traditions. Sometimes the best solutions come from surprising sources.

Protecting Homes, First Responders, and a City: San Diego Wildfires

A drought in 2007 left southern California particularly vulnerable to wildfires. Several naturally occurring and human-caused fires erupted and, due to extremely dry conditions and high winds, quickly spread. Southern California was ablaze and homes near San Diego were threatened. Thousands of firefighters fought the massive wildfires. Because the fires grew so rapidly, local firefighters were unable to contain the blazes. Federal and state agencies provided desperately needed assets to help manage the fire containment efforts. Not only were several homes destroyed and many areas evacuated, but the shifting winds and recurring backfires erupted in areas thought to be under control and threatened the lives of exhausted firefighting teams.

I participated as part of an unofficial covert team that came together because we shared frustration that the vast federal bureaucracy made it difficult to provide federal disaster assistance in a timely manner to assist local and state governments. Our team consisted of a Coast Guard helicopter pilot and innovator who deployed with me for Hurricane Katrina (Chris Kluckhuhn), a senior Air Force officer working for the Secretary of the Air Force (Steve "Hoog" Hoogasian), a civilian IT and systems expert working under contract for FEMA (Matt Kern), and me working at a think tank conducting research and analysis for DHS agencies.

Hoog intercepted an email to the Secretary of the Air Force from the local San Diego Emergency Command Center. They were desperately requesting that DOD provide infrared satellite imagery of wildfire sites so they could determine where backfires might erupt, which could trap firefighters and threaten neighborhoods. An earlier request for satellite imagery resulted in visual imagery and photos that only showed the massive smoke clouds over southern California and proved useless for detecting hot spots and potential backfires.

Hoog quickly engaged our unorthodox team for assistance. I mentioned the urgent need to several think-tank colleagues. One senior manager knew a NASA employee who was supporting the DHS Science and Technology Directorate and contacted him for ideas. The NASA employee replied that NASA already had an agreement with the National Fire Center in Boise, Idaho to provide infrared satellite imagery when needed. However, the San Diego Emergency Coordination Center didn't know this capability existed or how to get it. With a couple of phone calls, the National Fire Center quickly started sending infrared hotspot information to the San Diego Command Center coordinating firefighting efforts. Undoubtedly this information saved property and firefighters' lives. Sometimes we aren't aware of what *we* (collectively) already *know* to solve major problems!

Preparing for Disasters: A unique briefing for the Secretary of the Air Force

A year later, Hoog briefed the Secretary of the Air Force, senior Air Force officers, and officials on a wartime technology to accurately target enemy positions, weapons, and facilities for retribution. He titled the briefing "Unauthorized Progress," which I used (with his permission) in the title of this book. This visionary officer always looked to maximize opportunities. While his briefing focused on a wartime technical capability, he saw potential for this technology to assist local, state, and federal agencies with disaster response operations by targeting individuals and families needing rescue or immediate medical assistance. He asked our team to assist with developing the strategy and briefing details.

Chris and I provided details about how FEMA, federal, state, and local agencies attempted to share critical information, the importance of GIS systems and GPS capabilities, and accurate and timely information sharing from our Hurricane Katrina Command Center experience. Matt translated DOD capabilities into a parallel capability for disaster response operations replacing infantry, armored vehicles, tanks, and fighter jets with first responders, ambulances, fire and security vehicles, and rescue helicopters. Hoog orchestrated the briefing to address the required capability and test results for Air Force use, and then expanded the briefing to include the potential to provide a valuable capability to save lives in major disaster situations.

The briefing to the Secretary started with Hoog introducing a veteran in a wheelchair who explained that during his National Guard deployment to Afghanistan, his position was attacked, his buddy killed, and he lost his leg. Later they learned this "enemy" attack tragically occurred because of miscommunication that resulted in "friendly fire." He described how the new technology, using the proper protocols, would, to the maximum extent possible, prevent future friendly fire incidents.

Next, Hoog introduced Air Force and contractor technical experts who gave a virtual demonstration of the technology and an assessment of its capabilities to support Air Force wartime operations. Hoog then gave the briefing an unusual twist. "Mr. Secretary, I believe we've clearly demonstrated the capabilities of this new technology to be of great value to the Air Force in time of war. But there is a significant peacetime benefit for our nation for additional applications for disaster response." He then reintroduced the veteran in the wheelchair, revealing his role as an Oregon state trooper. In this capacity, the veteran explained how, when he and his team respond to severe storms and flooding in the Northwest, they need to quickly locate families trapped by mudslides and floodwaters. He described how the new technology could aid rescue services responding to natural disasters and prevent needless deaths.

Then Chris discussed the initial response operations for Hurricane Katrina. He described how this new technology could help rescuers locate people trapped in houses and rooftops, quickly identify damage to critical infrastructure, and more effectively mobilize emergency teams to save lives and property. Finally, he introduced Matt who described a plan to develop a peacetime disaster response use for the technology. Hoog ended the presentation with a request. "Mr. Secretary, in addition to the military applications, we've demonstrated the potential value of this technology for emergency disaster response. I hope you'll support our 'unauthorized progress' and ask you to share this technology with the DHS for their development and further use." The Secretary asked a few questions and was so impressed he told Hoog to prepare a letter for his signature to the Secretary of Homeland Security with a copy to the FEMA Administrator offering to share the technology. Sometimes proven solutions for one issue can be adapted and applied to address new and different challenges.

Radical Inclusion: You never know who will come up with that one suggestion, a different interpretation, or a vexing issue you haven't considered that can significantly enhance your solution or make you aware of major shortcomings. Wisdom can be obtained from elders who know the culture, someone with vital knowledge others aren't aware of, or a visionary who sees the potential for one problem's solution to solve other challenges. This intel gathered informally and in advance of making a formal proposal allows you time to make improvements to enhance your concept before it faces the tough scrutiny of decision makers.

Ironically, the action of humbly asking people who may have suggestions, or may be impacted either positively or negatively, for their candid reactions to your plan helps you gain critical support if you listen carefully, don't get defensive, and take the appropriate follow-up action. The process of searching out those you believe may have important information or ideas to consider and then asking their opinions, concerns, and insights is a sign of respect that's often rewarded with excellent suggestions. This is true whether it occurs in the mountains of Afghanistan, the hills outside of San Diego, or within the vast governmental bureaucracy that often doesn't know all its capabilities and fails to effectively connect the dots.

**Strategies for Radical Inclusion and Evolving
Your Initiative**

1. **Identify all key primary and secondary stakeholders** who may
   influence your initiative's success. Remember to include people
   who significantly influence decision makers and implementers.
   Don't minimize the impact of naysayers; understand their concerns and issues. To the extent possible, allay their concerns or
   develop a compelling explanation of why your initiative should
   proceed despite concerns. Maximize potential benefits of your
   initiatives based on input from those who would benefit.

2. **Clearly and concisely discuss your change initiative** by developing a thirty-second "elevator" speech succinctly explaining your initiative and a short but more detailed initiative
   description.

3. **Develop interview questions and engage stakeholders** so that
   you can better understand the issues, concerns, and opportunities associated with your initiative. Request the names of
   others whom the stakeholders believe could contribute to the
   discussion. Determine if you've overlooked anyone.

4. **Determine and prioritize the most essential stakeholder
   issues** by listening carefully for suggestions to improve your
   initiative (e.g., villagers relocating ancestors' graves to allow
   construction of a safer route for medical convoys). Consider
   using SWOT and "Importance versus Urgency" analyses
   (Chapter Three) to identify and prioritize actions to improve
   your initiative based on stakeholder feedback.

5. **Identify actions to improve your concept's potential for
   acceptance and support from stakeholders** by planning and
   implementing specific actions to improve your initiative.

Summary

> *The most important single ingredient in the formula of success is knowing how to get along with people.*
> ~ *Theodore Roosevelt*

This chapter discussed how to increase interest in your concept and gain stakeholder buy-in by learning the potential issues or concerns and the perceived opportunities with regard to your initiative. Once identified, you can prioritize issues and opportunities based on importance and urgency and create an action plan to improve your initiative.

Next *UP*: Identifying additional opportunities for your initiative and the risks you might encounter (organizational and personal) during implementation.

Chapter Six

Understanding Risks and Opportunities

If you want to make enemies, try to change something.
~ Woodrow Wilson

By now, you've identified and engaged key stakeholders to understand their issues, concerns, and potential benefits of your initiative. You've identified specific actions to take and prioritized them to mitigate perceived weaknesses or concerns about your initiative and maximize its benefits. But before you launch your mitigation and optimization efforts, you must consider the potential risks and opportunities:

- What resistance might you encounter, from whom, and why?
- What risks are associated with your initiative?
- What opportunities might be expanded upon?
- What additional opportunities might result from your initiative?

This next story illustrates how an initiative headed by a mid-grade federal employee experienced high-level risks and achieved incredible results.

David versus Goliath: How a Single Change Agent Takes on the Pentagon to Create a *Win-Win* Situation

In 1995, I served as commanding officer of the Civil Engineering Unit in Providence, Rhode Island. We were responsible for planning, constructing, maintaining, and renovating Coast Guard shore facilities in the Northeast. Our responsibilities also included real property and environmental activities. I inherited a terrific team of fifty-five dedicated professional men and women, civilians and active duty military, and the unit operated very smoothly. Shortly after I arrived, we received a copy of a letter to the Commandant from Senator Leahy of Vermont. He wrote about his concerns regarding Coast Guard batteries found on the lakebed near several navigational lights on Lake Champlain on the Vermont–New York border. My team investigated the allegations and found several 1960s vintage batteries next to most of the forty-two navigational lights on Lake Champlain. Coast Guard maintenance teams discarded the sixty-pound batteries in the 1960s and early 1970s. Safely removing heavy batteries onboard a small boat bouncing on the waves can be treacherous and some teams took the easy way out by leaving the batteries at their sites. In the early 1970s, the Environmental Protection Agency (EPA) declared mercury to be an environmental hazard. Since these batteries contained minute amounts of mercury, they needed to be removed.

Senator Leahy rightfully wanted to know what the Coast Guard planned to do. My team quickly developed a game plan to remove the batteries. They prepared an extensive project description (about one and one-half inches thick!) with detailed environmental testing. They planned to use a contracting mechanism established for minority contractors to expedite the contract award process. The project involved removing all the batteries over three years (fourteen sites per year) for $240,000. I found the *financial risk* unacceptably high—too much money for too little results—and believed we could do much better for the taxpayers. Earlier, while assigned in the Great Lakes, I contracted a small diving company to remove batteries at forty-five navigation lights on the St. Mary's River on the Michigan–Canadian border for much less, and I knew the Coast Guard had partnered with Army and Navy dive teams in the Gulf of Mexico to recover navigational batteries. I directed my team to find a quicker and more cost-effective way to remove the batteries. The project leader, Luke Dlhopolsky, a quiet, professional GS-12 environmental specialist, led the project. In the meantime, Senator Leahy wrote another letter to the Commandant demanding action.

Luke quickly went to work. He checked the availability of Navy and Army dive teams along the Atlantic Coast and found an available Army dive team out of Fort Eustis, Virginia willing to perform the work if we would cover their expenses, which we gladly did. Luke lined up the dive team with the local Coast Guard unit and the battery recovery project got underway.

The work finished just before the October storm season began. The dive team, working with local Coasties, did an incredible job. They surveyed and removed batteries from *all forty-two sites* on the lake at a total cost of $60,000, *one-fourth the contracting estimate, in one-third the time*. We awarded project participants a Coast Guard Team Commendation ribbon, including our Army colleagues. Senator Leahy sent three letters of gratitude and appreciation to our unit, the local Coast Guard unit, and the Commandant. Luke led and executed a win-win situation, even overcoming *technical risk* when the Coast Guard boat became inoperable.

But the story doesn't end there. Luke was a smart guy and thought about other opportunities to use DOD dive teams to recover batteries alongside coastal navigational lights. He developed a seven-year plan to recover all the batteries along the New England coast. Remarkably, Luke lined up ten Army and Navy dive teams to help Coast Guard units clean up the coast the first year. They considered this a no-cost training opportunity to develop their teams, while serving the nation. Luke took the Lake Champlain win-win scenario to a much higher, more strategic level!

Then a strange thing happened. Two weeks after Luke lined up the dive teams, a master chief diver called stating, "I'm terribly sorry, Mr. Dlhopolsky, but I've been informed there's a Pentagon policy prohibiting us from assisting the Coast Guard in recovering navigation batteries. I'm afraid we won't be able to help as planned." Within days, Luke received similar calls from other dive teams.

Luke came into my office and told me the bad news. We were both frustrated. I asked him, "Does this make sense to you? I know Army and Navy dive teams, like the one used on Lake Champlain often help the Coast Guard, including recovering batteries. Something doesn't make sense." I asked him to get the Pentagon policy in writing so we could see what it said.

Luke came back the next day and said, "I've got good news and bad news. The good news is a formal Pentagon policy prohibiting DOD dive units from assisting us with recovering navigational batteries doesn't exist. However, I spoke with the DOD diving operations policy makers and they directed units not to assist the Coast Guard because of a ten-year-old disagreement between Navy and Coast Guard divers. They went on to say that if we didn't like their policy, we can write a letter to the Chief of Naval Operations (CNO), a four-star admiral, to see if we can get it overturned." This seemed to be an arrogant remark from some rather smug bureaucrats, especially in light of the dive teams' willingness to help and an opportunity for free training. I asked Luke to contact Coast Guard headquarters to have one of our senior staff speak with the Pentagon diving policy staff. Unfortunately, they had no luck impacting the decision.

Neither Luke nor I could have foreseen this *political risk* in advance. We often worked as partners with our sister services. We had a choice. We could back down and go the standard contracting route that would take much longer, cost much more, and result in further degradation of the environment until a contractor removed the batteries, or we could take the action we believed to be in the best interest of the nation and American taxpayers by assuming the risk of senior leaders shutting us down. Luke and I discussed our options and decided to draft a letter to the CNO. Now we weren't arrogant or foolish enough to send the letter directly to the CNO ourselves. Instead, Luke prepared a letter, which I reviewed and forwarded to a two-star admiral at Coast Guard headquarters, who sent it to his counterpart at the Pentagon. Then we waited for a response.

A curious thing happened. We never did receive a response to our letter. However, two weeks later, Luke received a call from Panama City, Florida. "Mr. Dlhopolsky, I'm the master chief in charge of a forty-person Navy dive team, and I understand you need some assistance. If you need any help at all, including recovery of navigation batteries, my team would be happy to help you." In the days that followed, Luke received more calls of assistance from additional dive teams. While no one mentioned the letter, Luke and I suspected that a sharp staff officer had read the letter and spoke to a senior leader who may have said something like, "Why wouldn't we help the Coast Guard if we have the capacity, they provide the funding, and it helps the environment? Find a way to help them out without acknowledging an idiotic policy that never formally existed!"

Luke worked diligently with the DOD dive teams and local Coast Guard units to clean up the vast majority of battery sites in *only three years (instead of the original seven-year plan!), saving millions of dollars* while accelerating cleanup of the coastal environment. It was truly a win-win situation, led by someone who did the right thing, had the courage to *lead from the middle*, thought strategically to identify broader opportunities, and persevered despite real and potential risks. Luke is a modest professional and would say instead of having "courage to lead from the middle" that he was just too stubborn to let a good deal (Army and Navy divers) be tossed aside without questioning a policy that didn't make sense. He's a terrific example of an ordinary dedicated professional doing his job to the best of his abilities and achieving *extraordinary* results!

Risks

As demonstrated in the above story, risks may be technical, financial, or political and may impact, not just the organization, but you personally. It's important to understand them so you can manage your and others' expectations and make contingency plans (e.g., *Plan B*) in case Plan A doesn't work. Chapters Eight (Implementation) and Nine (Learning from Failure) discuss risks in more detail. It's important to understand the type of risk, its source (individuals, competing organizations, implementing new technology), and whether the risk is limited to just impacting the initiative's success, or if it may impact the organization's reputation and decision makers', implementers', or your credibility.

The Risk of *Wild Success*

You should also understand the potential impact if your initiative is *wildly successful*. I've experienced *near-failure due to wild success* a couple times and found it be strange and counterintuitive.

While chairing the Coast Guard's Innovation Council, we attempted to expand participation at the annual Innovation Expo. The first Expo held at the Coast Guard Academy in 2001 had thirty-five booths and two hundred participants. The second Expo, at Baltimore's Inner Harbor, had sixty-five booths and five hundred participants. We were happy with the growth and decided to have the third Expo at Inner Harbor but didn't anticipate *wild success* and its potential impact. That year attendance grew to one hundred booths and nine hundred participants. The fire marshal almost shut the Expo down for exceeding capacity of the hotel's ballrooms. One private sector vendor said, "Tickets to the Coast Guard Innovation Expo are harder to obtain than tickets to the Preakness horse race." It just so happened that the Preakness was being held that week in Baltimore too. The next week I learned the Argentine Embassy was upset because the fire marshal denied their staff access to the Expo. I didn't even know Argentina was interested in attending!

Consider what might happen if your change initiative wildly succeeds. Would you have enough staff or supplies to meet an overwhelming demand for your product or services? How could you manage expectations? What could be the impact and how might you lessen the negative aspects while emphasizing to leaders the successful components of your initiative?

The DHS Risk Model:

DHS conducts significant research on the risk of a bad event occurring, whether it's a terrorist attack or a natural or manmade disaster. DHS models the probability and impact of *bad events* so it can take preventative measures to alleviate negative impacts. A generalized early model defined *Risk* as a function of three factors: *Threat, Vulnerability, and Consequence*, or simply stated:

Risk = Threat x Vulnerability x Consequence

- **Risk** is the impact of a negative event (in dollars)
- **Threat** is a probability factor from 0.0 (no threat) to 1.0 (definite threat with a high likelihood of occurrence). Note: For a terrorist incident, *Threat* is a function of a terrorist organization's *intent* to conduct a terrorist act and its *capability* to do harm
- **Vulnerability** is a probability factor from 0.0 (no vulnerability) to 1.0 (highly vulnerable)
- **Consequence** is the negative impact of an attack or natural/manmade disaster (in dollars)

The model provided a broad understanding of the most significant threats such as hurricanes, earthquakes, and terrorist attacks. The model also proved useful when DHS elected to provide grants to reduce the risks and impact of bad events. While not perfect, the DHS Risk Model helped assess the likelihood and impact of a potential bad event.

The Opportunity Model:

If we can model and assess *Risk*, the likelihood and impact of a *negative* event happening, we should be able to turn the model upside down to model *Opportunity*, the likelihood and potential impact of a *positive* event. To convert the *Risk Model* into an *Opportunity Model*, we replace *Risk* with *Opportunity Factor* and replace the *Consequence* of a bad event with the *Benefit* of a potential good outcome. The *Threat* of a terrorist event, which was a function of terrorists' intent and capability to execute an attack, is replaced with *Intent* and *Capability* of an innovator and her/his organization to implement a beneficial change. The *Intent (I)* and *Capability (C)* factors are probabilities (0.0 - 1.0) described below, and their product (I x C) determines the *Probability of Success (POS)*. This Opportunity Model can be described as:

> **Opportunity Factor (OPP)** = Total Potential Benefit (B) x Probability of Success (POS), where
>
> POS = Intent (I) x Capability (C)

- **Opportunity Factor** is the likely benefit of a positive event (in dollars).

- **Total Potential Benefit (B)** is the positive impact of a change initiative (in dollars or converted to dollars for beneficial outcomes such as reduced process cycle time, new capabilities, improved customer satisfaction/commitment, etc.).

- **Probability of Success** is the probability (0.0 – 1.0) the change initiative will be successfully implemented. POS is composed of two factors, the *Intent* to adopt the initiative, and the *Capability* to successfully implement the change.

- **Intent** is an estimated probability of the organization's desire and commitment *overall* to adopt the change, ranging from 0.0 (weak/ no intent) to 1.0 (strong commitment to the change initiative). This includes a commitment of primary stakeholders, key support offices, suppliers, and possibly the legal office, perhaps the union, and, ultimately, the decision makers. What is the organization's overall commitment to adopt the change? Will it provide the support, resources, staff, and policy changes needed for success?

- **Capability** is an estimated probability of the competence and ability to successfully implement the change initiative, ranging from 0.0 (no capability exists) to 1.0 (the implementation team clearly has the competence and experience to succeed). Does the organization have staff with the right experience, skills, training, and education to successfully implement proposed changes? If not, is it willing to bring in external expertise to assist with the implementation? Has it successfully implemented similar changes previously?

The Total Potential Benefit is the value if the initiative is totally successful. Depending on the type of beneficial outcome achieved, *Benefit* may be measured in total dollars for a one-time event or in dollars per year for recurring events such as reducing the process cycle time. When determining the *Total Potential Benefit*, think beyond the pilot project to include the total number of locations, people, processes, etc. which might be beneficially impacted once the initiative proves itself, just like Luke expanding the battery recovery project model to all New England, once it proved effective on Lake Champlain.

 Strategies

1. **Understand risks to reputation and implementation; mitigate the risks.** Risks may be technical, financial, or political and reflect upon the organization as a whole, a major division, and/or you personally. Some risks are obvious and others unanticipated. To the extent possible, understand the risks and work to minimize their potential impact.

2. **Explore additional beneficial opportunities for your initiative.** Who else might benefit and how? Think beyond your pilot or initial project, can you expand the initial beneficial results to reap additional positive outcomes?

3. **Understand the Opportunity Model as a tool to assess potential benefits of your initiative**. Maximize the potential for future benefits. Explore and understand what may limit your organization's *Intent* (commitment) and *Capability* to implement your initiative.

4. **Know how to apply the Opportunity Model to assess and compare various solution concepts for your idea/challenge.** Be able to identify the solution concept with the greatest likely return on investment.

Summary

Nothing in life is to be feared, it is only to be understood. Now is the time to understand more, so that we may fear less. ~ Dr. Marie Curie

This chapter focused on the risks and opportunities encountered when initiating change. Luke Dlhopolsky remarkably overcame several serious risks, including being shut down by the Pentagon, and sought expanded opportunities for his initiative to remove disposed batteries from coastal navigational lights across New England, ultimately saving millions of dollars, accomplishing a seven-year project plan in only three years, and protecting the environment. The *Opportunity Model* is a useful tool to assess and compare solution concepts that we can apply to determine which concept has the greatest likely return on investment.

Next UP: Leaping the hurdles to concept acceptance—explores six common reasons proposed initiatives are not implemented. Also, the startup of the Coast Guard's Innovation Program that was designed to overcome barriers to the transformation of creative ideas into reality.

Chapter 7

ENERGIZING THE ENTERPRISE

The best way to predict the future is to create it.
~ Abraham Lincoln

You've taken your idea, improved it with the insight of key stake-holders, considered where the risks are, and identified the potential opportunities. Now you need to convince decision makers to let you implement your idea and pilot test the concept. They'll decide whether to proceed given the circumstances: the importance and urgency of your challenge, the likelihood your concept will succeed, the availability of time and resources needed to implement your solution and competing demands and opportunities for the required resources. This is an exciting, yet apprehensive time in the change process. Once you gain your leaders' support for implementation, you're committed to going forward. There's no going back!

This chapter won't tell you how to implement your initiative, which depends on your specific change solution. Rather, it provides guidance to obtain decision makers' approval to proceed with implementation. First, we'll discuss six reasons ideas aren't accepted for implementation. Then we'll examine a major initiative startup, the Coast Guard's Innovation Program.

Why Ideas Aren't Accepted for Implementation

I've seen hundreds of new ideas and initiatives with the Coast Guard's Innovation Program and as commanding officer of the Coast Guard Research and Development Center. Although decision makers decide *not* to proceed with change initiatives for many reasons, there's one primary reason good leaders support promising change initiatives: their belief that the initiative will ultimately provide a good return on investment and benefit the organization. Sometimes the benefits are tangible as in cost savings or reduction in the process cycle time, and sometimes the benefits are intangible as in the safety of a community with good law enforcement protection or an innovative company spirit leading to the discovery of new products.

I found the reasons innovative ideas weren't pursued fell into six broad categories:

1. Insufficient Research
2. Under/Poorly Communicated
3. Insufficient Benefit
4. Competing Priorities
5. Too Much Risk
6. Internal Politics

You may note the similarities between the various reasons that ideas aren't pursued for implementation and Chapter Four's major factors considered by decision makers when deciding whether or not to support change initiative concepts. The primary difference is the stakes are much higher when you start implementation. Management is now dedicating resources, staff hours, and overhead to your project and senior leadership or key customers may have made commitments anticipating your initiative's success. If it isn't successful, this may be viewed as wasted effort and your credibility, as well as your supporters' credibility, may be damaged. The risks increase significantly.

Insufficient Research: If an initiative isn't completely flushed out, the potential for major technical flaws increases exponentially and could lead to an unworkable solution. Or there may be insufficient information to convince decision makers the initiative is a good investment. Often a change initiative isn't the first attempt to overcome a specific challenge, and lessons learned from prior experience and failure must be considered. Decision makers aware of prior efforts expect you to consider what others tried before. Loss of credibility due to a lack of thorough preparation is hard to overcome.

Under/Poorly Communicated: If you don't communicate your idea well, it's not likely to be accepted. Symptoms of under/poor communication include: a lack of awareness of the initiative among potential supporters; uninformed naysayers exaggerating risks and downsides; and unfounded doubts about the potential for success due to incorrect, incomplete, or confusing communications.

Insufficient Benefit: Some ideas don't generate a sense of urgency for implementation, prove difficult to find sponsors to support them, and may require resources that aren't readily available. While the idea may generate an improvement, the improvement isn't significant enough for decision makers to provide staff or resources for implementation.

Competing Priorities: Your idea may not be chosen for implementation because it's simply one of many good ideas for which there are limited resources. Or, it may be a good idea, but in a larger context it may be perceived as negatively impacting the big picture by potentially derailing higher priority initiatives. The bottom line is your initiative may be perceived as having too high of an opportunity cost to compete with already planned initiatives.

Opportunity cost is the difference between the value resulting from using resources for your initiative and the highest and best use of those resources. For instance, you may need two staff and $100,000 for your initiative, which is expected to return a value of one million dollars.

If your initiative is competing against another with the same resource requirements with an expected return of three million dollars, the opportunity cost is the difference between the expected outcomes, two million dollars. You want your initiative to have the highest possible return on investment relative to other options.

Too Much Risk: The benefits aren't perceived as outweighing the risks. If decision makers feel there's too much risk to the organization, or personal risk for decision makers or implementers, your initiative is likely to be rejected. Another situation may involve working in a no-risk or risk-averse culture where any change to the status quo may be difficult to convince decision makers to agree to.

Internal Politics: This can be the most challenging and frustrating category you encounter. Symptoms include not being able to meet with and/or be heard by decision makers; attempting to move forward with your initiative when your first- or second-level supervisor isn't a supporter; petty jealousies within the workplace; the not-invented-here syndrome; key players threatened by your initiative; turf issues; or your initiative is perceived as impacting a dicey political issue. These symptoms can result in obstacles as you attempt to implement your idea.

Now let's look at an enterprise-wide initiative to help change agents overcome these hurdles.

The Coast Guard Innovation Program

In 2002, I started a new assignment as Chief of the Office of Quality and Management Effectiveness working for the Chief of Staff and Vice Commandant at Coast Guard headquarters. In addition to leading the Coast Guard's Quality Program and coordinating senior leadership conferences, my responsibilities included implementing and evolving the Coast Guard's new Innovation Program. Vice-Commandant, Vice Admiral Tom Collins initiated an Innovation Council a year earlier to identify, leverage, and jumpstart excellent ideas developed by personnel at all levels to improve organizational performance.

Vice Admiral Collins envisioned the Innovation Program conducting an annual Expo to highlight great work initiated across the Coast Guard. We held the first Innovation Expo at the Coast Guard Academy in Connecticut in 2001. Over two hundred Coast Guard employees and Academy cadets visited the thirty-five innovation exhibits. The booths were not highly sophisticated, but the Expo built the foundation for the *innovation community* within the Coast Guard.

We held the second Expo at Baltimore's Inner Harbor with all booths and exhibits presented by Coast Guard personnel, but the private sector was invited to observe and learn about Coast Guard mission requirements and innovative solutions Coasties developed and implemented. It was a huge success with over five hundred participants and sixty-five exhibits. Coast Guard Headquarters program managers from Washington and a few admirals attended, including Vice Admiral Collins, selected to be the next commandant.

Over the next year, with my two-person innovation staff and the Commandant's Innovation Council (fifteen senior staff and part-time contributors), we thought about the challenge of integrating innovation, initiative, and *leading from the middle* within a hierarchical organization. Our strengths included strong support from top leadership and several creative and energetic thought leaders in our group. Our weakness was that there were very few of us on the Innovation Council to make a significant constructive impact on the entire organization and its culture. We needed effective strategies to serve as force-multipliers to magnify the impact of innovation.

One strategy involved recognizing creative Coast Guard innovators as role models for their colleagues. We created the Innovation Awards to recognize the achievements of constructive change agents in three areas: Operations and Readiness; Science and Technology; and Support, Training and Administration. We had a dilemma in that we could reward civilians with cash bonuses, but not their military colleagues. Likewise, we could give military members medals, but not their civilian peers. Ultimately, we decided the best strategy included publicly recognizing individuals with a plaque presented by the Commandant, listing winners' names in a message sent to all Coast Guard units, and having the Commandant provide $10,000 to each award winner's unit for encouraging and supporting an environment where innovative solutions could flourish.

In 2003, the Commandant gave the necessary permission to hold the Flag Conference and the Innovation Expo together. This opportunity provided senior military and civilian executives the chance to meet innovators and exhibitors, learn about their issues and solutions, and enjoy an evening at a joint reception for participants. We opened the Expo to private sector solution providers to demonstrate their capabilities, give them the opportunity to better understand Coast Guard challenges and issues, and reduce Coast Guard exhibitor costs. We held the 2003 Expo again at Baltimore's Inner Harbor and attendance grew to nine hundred participants with over one hundred exhibits. Due to the great turnout, the fire marshal nearly shut us down for exceeding the fire safety capacity of the hotel's ballrooms and exhibit hall. We planned for every failure mode, except wild success!

The next year, we made two additional changes to continue to grow support for an innovative culture throughout the Coast Guard. We added an additional category to the Innovation Awards for management improvements. We also initiated Innovation Scholarships for Coast Guard personnel pursuing a specific one-year master's degree in Quality Systems Management that included a process improvement project to enhance organizational performance. These $2,000 scholarships, combined with tuition assistance, made it possible for interested personnel to obtain a master's degree in twelve months for under $4,000 while gaining recognition for improving the organization. In fact, students didn't receive their degrees until they could prove a positive return on investment for their projects, including their tuition costs!

In 2004, we moved the Expo to a larger venue to avoid space and capacity challenges. We chose a new international exhibition center in historic Savannah, Georgia. Attendance increased again from nine hundred to fourteen hundred participants and over two hundred exhibits. My staff used the Innovation Expo as an opportunity to have our annual conference for twenty-three Quality Performance Consultants, and Reserve Training Center Yorktown invited their class of international students from over twenty countries to attend the Expo. As we reviewed the list of attendees, we noticed several Coast Guard communities were represented: aviators, ship-drivers, engineers, information technologists, training and education staff, etc. We also found local hotels that were willing to give us meeting rooms at no charge due to all the rooms being booked by Expo participants.

To further expand the innovation culture, we promoted a new strategy. Many Coast Guard communities held annual conferences to share current policies, training, lessons learned, and best practices. We decided to promote the Innovation Expo as the *gathering place* for various Coast Guard communities by offering free conference rooms for any community that would hold their annual conference with the Expo. The advantages included travel fund savings, since many would attend the Expo anyway, no-cost conference rooms, and opportunities to include guest speakers (also attending the Expo) such as executive leaders.

We held the 2005 Expo in Silicon Valley, California, concurrently with the Flag Conference again, and had fifteen hundred participants and nearly three hundred exhibits. The quality and sophistication of Coast Guard exhibits improved substantially over the years as they sought to replicate the high quality of the private sector booths. In addition, federal Coast Guard partners were offered opportunities to exhibit including DHS and DOD organizations. Throughout this period, we ensured at least forty percent of the exhibits were Coast Guard innovators to maintain the focus on the Coast Guard mission and support requirements.

Chief of Staff, Vice Admiral Thad Allen, a strong innovation advo-cate, became Commandant in 2006, and formalized the connection between the annual Innovation Expo and the fall Flag Conference, announcing they would be co-located during his tenure as Com-mandant. Expo participation continued to grow to twenty-five hun-dred by 2011 and included over four hundred booths. The number of Innovation Award nominations grew to over sixty per year, and *over seven hundred Coast Guard personnel earned master's degrees in Quality Systems Management while producing projects valued by Coast Guard senior champions at over $500 million.* During 2001 to 2011, the Coast Guard developed an innovation culture that encouraged critical creative thinking and ideas on both an individual and organizational level. This culture prepared the Coast Guard to respond effectively and quickly to new crises never previously encountered such as Hurricane Katrina and the Deepwater Horizon oil spill.

What made the Innovation Program, and specifically Coast Guard innovators, successful? Let's take a closer look.

Most Coast Guard Innovation Award nominees were *experts in their field*, often frontline workers, and closest to the process or most impacted by the issue or challenge. They demonstrated a *bias for action* by initiating activities to mitigate problems or seize opportunities. The Innovation Council leveraged its *senior champion*, Vice Admiral Col-lins, while Vice Commandant, to modify an ongoing contract to make Coast Guard operational data available so units could measure perfor-mance. Despite significant pushback from senior acquisition staff, the *senior champion* intervened to modify the contract.

While Coast Guard Innovation Award winners were primarily concerned with *the little picture*, solving workplace problems, at the R&D Center and for broad initiatives, we also had to consider the *big strategic picture*—what unintended consequences may occur as a result of our solution? What other opportunities might develop due to our new initiative? In all initiatives seeking innovation funds, the investment in terms of time, staffing, equipment, and funding had to make sense for the organization. The gain had to exceed the cost and a *business case* had to be made prior to approval and implementation. Likewise, the Innovation Council *tracked performance metrics* to see if our actions contributed to creating an innovative culture. We reviewed how the Expo attendance and number of exhibits increased over time, noted the growing number of Innovation Award nominations, and, perhaps most tellingly, saw the Innovation category of the Office of Personnel Management (OPM) annual employee survey increase by a significant six percentage points.

The Innovation Council and staff did a remarkable job *mitigating potential failure modes* of Innovation Expos but still were *caught off-guard twice due to wild success.*

The Innovation Council further expanded the culture of innovation by encouraging and incentivizing professional development through a master's program in Quality Systems Management which required a master's level process improvement project and experiential learning. *The program bootlegged resources* by leveraging the agency's tuition assistance program and added an Innovation Scholarship to jumpstart the program and encourage early adapters to become not only educated, but proficient at leading constructive change efforts.

The Innovation Program also benefited from an insightful and *highly effective marketing program.* By introducing annual Innovation Awards presented by the Commandant and combining the Innovation Expo with the Flag Conference, we successfully changed the image of both events by employing the concept of the gathering place for annual events. Coast Guard employees eagerly looked forward to the Expo, and both attendance and exhibit numbers grew rapidly.

Many Innovation Award winners started their initiatives with *proof of concept pilot tests and prototypes* and quickly adapted the lessons learned and opportunities identified during field tests to increase the value of their ideas to the organization.

After the 9/11 terrorist attacks, Vice Admiral Thad Allen, Atlantic Area Commander at the time, called me at the R&D Center *to team with his operational experts* to assess risks in our nation's major maritime ports. I teamed our operational support engineers, scientists, and specialists with Admiral Allen's operational experts and a *third-party company* recognized as one of the best in risk identification and management, to develop a risk assessment tool for our ports. We jointly developed this tool and used it to identify the highest risk factors in major U.S. ports.

Assertive strategies, although used less often and riskier, can also be effective. The Maine lighthouse initiative (Chapter Three) was one of those situations. While the Coast Guard transferred lighthouses through legislation in the past, it was typically one lighthouse at a time. My real property specialist at Civil Engineering Unit Providence, Ted, knew Coast Guard lawyers would be nervous about the potential transfer of multiple lighthouses, as it had never been done before, would prove complex, and require a lot of work. Yet the benefits of successfully transferring ownership of the lighthouses would save millions of taxpayer dollars in maintenance and renovation costs. We decided to *partner* quietly with the requesting nonprofit organization and see what might develop. If something looked promising, we'd let headquarters know, but only after we had a definite implementable plan in place. In other words, we *worked under the radar.*

As commanding officer, I received a few calls from the head of the civil engineering program stating they heard rumors of possible legislation to transfer lighthouses. I replied we just responded to questions about acquiring lighthouses and would let headquarters know if anything definite appeared likely. Because of the complexity of the process and the huge potential benefit if we succeeded, *I was prepared to beg forgiveness after the fact, rather than ask permission, which I knew would be denied.* A week before Senator Snowe introduced an amendment to allow transfer of up to thirty-six light-houses, we informed headquarters about the forthcoming legislation. I was prepared to be chastised for not engaging headquarters' staff earlier in the process, but it never happened. Apparently, Senator Snowe let the Commandant know the excitement she and the entire state of Maine felt anticipating the lighthouse transfers! A year later, both Maine senators and the Senate Appropriations Committee Chairman joined the Coast Guard Commandant in Rockland, Maine for the ceremony celebrating the transfer of twenty-eight lighthouses to qualified organizations.

 Strategies

Three strategies to overcome the six hurdles towards getting support to implement your initiative include:

1. **Be *the* expert on your initiative,** know how it will truly benefit your organization, the realistic (not exaggerated) risks, and its vulnerabilities. Be able to answer any questions and demonstrate you've given considerable thought to any potential negative aspects.

2. **Understand your organization and key players** and how your initiative may impact them. Build strong support from those who see the value and will benefit from your efforts. Mitigate concerns of others to the extent possible. Be aware of internal politics that may impact your initiative and competing priorities.

3. **Effectively communicate** why your initiative should be implemented in the near future by building a compelling case for action. Clearly convey the value of your initiative and attempt to establish a *sense of urgency* to implement your idea.

Summary

The secret of change is to focus all of your energy, not on changing the old, but on building the new.
~ Socrates

This chapter focused on six primary hurdles your change initiative must overcome to be accepted for implementation. It also outlined an enterprise-wide initiative to help change agents, at all levels, leap over these hurdles to initiate constructive change to improve organizational performance. Several actions and strategies used to initiate the Coast Guard's Innovation Program are described.

Next *UP:* Implementing your change initiative. *Making it real* with twelve strategies for overcoming potential showstoppers and implementing your initiative.

Chapter Eight

Implementation Strategies

*The moment one definitely commits oneself, then
providence moves too. All sorts of things occur to help
one that would never otherwise have occurred. . . .
Whatever you can do or dream you can, begin it.
Boldness has genius, power, and magic in it.
Begin it now. - Attributed to Goethe*

This chapter introduces twelve strategies to move your initiative through the presentation and implementation phases. You can apply some strategies more effectively in certain circumstances, and Table 8.1 suggests specific strategies for addressing common reasons decision makers choose not to implement ideas.

Lessons Learned, Potential Showstoppers, and Helpful Strategies

In Chapter Seven, we examined six reasons why ideas aren't accepted or implemented:

1. Insufficient Research
2. Under/Poorly Communicated
3. Insufficient Benefit
4. Competing Priorities

5. Too Much Risk

6. Internal Politics

I've witnessed several successful strategies that innovators use to avoid or reduce the likelihood of these potential showstoppers. Common strategies for successfully implementing change initiatives, shown below, may be used independently or in combinations most appropriate for your situation.

1. **Become an Expert:** Don't just be *an* expert on your issue; become *the expert*, the go-to person. Know more about your challenge than anyone else. If you can't become the expert, identify who is and engage them. Ask for their insights and advice. Request that they become advocates of your initiative, since having their support will give you significant credibility when you present your idea to decision makers. Plus, you'll be able to address any questions because you will either know the answers or know where to find the answers.

2. **Demonstrate a "Bias for Action":** In his book, *In Search of Excellence*, Tom Peters describes one distinguishing characteristic of successful and agile firms as their "bias for action." These firms are willing to move ahead with actions even when they don't have all the information desired. In this scenario, the decision makers don't make choices based solely on an objective factual analysis and the best business case. They're often also influenced by the credibility and track record of the person making the recommendations. This means a good business case might exist, but decision makers will have concerns about implementation of the initiative if the individual making the recommendation has historically not followed through. However, if you have credibility as an effective change agent, a bias for action that has shown positive results, they're more likely

to have confidence in you, even if your business case isn't as strong as desired. Your credibility can influence decision makers to accept your proposal and can prove especially valuable when competing for limited resources.

3. **Find a Sponsor or Champion:** An excellent strategy for cutting bureaucratic red tape and expediting your initiative is to find someone who will make your case and advocate on your behalf. This strategy involves approaching the people who strongly influence the decision maker, presenting your idea and convincing them it's beneficial to the organization, and then having them take it to the decision maker. Be prepared to answer their questions because the decision maker will likely ask their opinion of you and your initiative. If you've already addressed their concerns, shown the potential benefit of your idea, and demonstrated how it can be successfully implemented, they're likely to support you. With a senior champion's backing, many people who'd raise issues to sidetrack your efforts, slow you down, or stop you, won't challenge you. This can help when dealing with competing priorities, perceived risk, and internal politics.

4. **Third Party Intervention/Assistance:** Sometimes others may perceive your passion to address significant challenges as overly optimistic, underestimating difficulties, and not grounded in reality. It can seem no matter what you say, your points are discounted and have no impact. This can be frustrating, negatively impact your confidence, and derail your bias for action. Many change agents overcome this potential showstopper by asking a credible, unbiased expert to review their proposal and present it to decision makers. The expert stands a much better chance of convincing decision makers to consider your proposal seriously because they'll be seen as knowledgeable and objective.

Third party experts are familiar with the latest research and are often polished presenters who will clearly communicate your initiative's potential and may effectively minimize or mitigate concerns about risks. While it may be frustrating to rely on someone else to present your initiative, you increase your odds of success by taking advantage of this strategy. Know that in time, your credibility will increase because of the success of your ideas.

5. **Take a Systems Approach:** Understand both the *big* and *little* pictures. Multiple perspectives surrounding complex issues can result in conflicting positions. Learn others' perspectives on your issue. Don't be so wedded to your position that you ignore a key stakeholder's *truth* or their perspective. Multiple parties can be right based on their position. Differences often occur due to different functions: direct operations or support, dealing with tactical issues, broader operational issues, or far-ranging strategic issues. Both the little picture, immediate and direct issues, and the big picture, broader strategic concerns are important for you to anticipate 1) what you really need to do, and 2) what information you need to make wise decisions. Those many levels above the process won't know the precise details like those closest to it. Be sure to include knowledge and perspectives from those closer to the process because it's often essential to make the best decisions. To achieve success, you need to reduce the perceptions others may have of the high risks for your initiative, ensure you don't negatively impact other high priorities, and carefully navigate through internal politics.

6. **Build the Business Case:** A strong business case is critical for success and helps market your concept to key players. Managers want to know the business case for initiatives requiring

additional staff, equipment, or funding. You must demonstrate how the organization will receive a valuable return on investment and substantiate that the benefits will be well worth the costs of time, staff, equipment, and funding needed. Benefits can be tangible, e.g., cost savings, or intangible, such as improving morale or safety. Benefits typically include cost savings, providing a new or enhanced capability, or improving efficiency by reducing process cycle time. Steps for building a strong business case include sharing data showing existing performance doesn't meet desired goals, tracking key performance metrics, flowcharting processes, and removing duplicate and low-value actions. A strong business case can demonstrate why your idea's value exceeds the benefits of competing initiatives.

7. **Network/Team/Partner for Success:** In Chapter Five, we discussed networking and teaming with key players to gain critical buy-in and create a critical mass of support for your initiative. Two strategies to build support include the "Law of Reciprocity" and "saving the willing first." Dr. Robert Cialdini, Professor Emeritus at Arizona State University, describes the "Law of Reciprocity" in his best-selling book *Influence: The Psychology of Persuasion*. In nearly every culture, if a person freely provides a favor, gift, or helpful service to someone, that party feels obligated to return the favor. This same strategy can apply within organizations. If you support others, they may assist and support you in the future.

A complementary strategy is to find early adopters, those most likely to see the benefits of your initiative and gain their support early on—the saving the willing first strategy. This strategy helps in several ways: 1) it gains early supporters who positively communicate your change initiative to others; 2) you can practice and improve your message delivery; 3) you increase confidence you will be successful; and 4) you don't use significant energy and emotion early on with hard sells. Networking, teaming, and partnering helps communicate your message, convinces others of your initiative's value, and establishes that your idea should be considered a priority when competing for scarce resources. This strategy can also help with internal politics.

8. **Plan for Every Failure Mode:** This strategy includes leveraging your harshest critics' issues to improve your initiative and implementation plan. Listen objectively to criticisms of your initiative and determine which may be truly detrimental and how you can eliminate or mitigate these concerns. Consider what you need for success and the options you have if those components aren't available. For instance, two backup options may be to either conduct a smaller scale pilot test of your initiative or plan a phased implementation. One often overlooked scenario is foreseeing the potential consequences if your initiative wildly succeeds. How would this impact staffing, suppliers, space, time to delivery, etc.? You should link this strategy to your "Build the Business Case" strategy.

9. **Meeting Resource Requirements:** While I was an Excellence in Government Fellow, we benchmarked 3M in Minneapolis for innovation. Much of 3M's success is due to their innovative culture and talented engineers and scientists who successfully developed five hundred new products annually. 3M gives their engineers and scientists fifteen percent of their time to think about and work on new products not necessarily associated with their current assignments. They partner with peers, and managers provide a small budget to support the most promising ideas. 3M innovators convince colleagues of their ideas' potential, gain support, evolve their ideas, and then take them to managers for innovation funds to conduct a pilot test. 3M calls the process

"bootlegging," with many ideas worked on simultaneously. The best ideas percolate to the top. This includes their famous "Post-It Note" invention, initially a failed product until one 3M employee showed the potential use for post-it notes in the office. While your organization may not have an innovation fund, you may find other resources to support your initiative start-up through perhaps end-of-year funds, related projects, or training funds.

Another strategy involves partnering and sharing the resource burden with another part of the organization or external partner who may benefit from the initiative. Finally, if you can't get all the resources needed for full implementation, but have some initial support, consider phasing the implementation plan. This allows more time to build support and prove your initiative's value.

10. **Develop an Effective Marketing Strategy:** To get your initiative accepted for implementation, you need an effective marketing strategy. You researched your idea and discussed it with key stakeholders to better understand the benefits, costs, opportunities, and concerns. But to gain approval for implementation, you must gain access to decision makers, obtain their buy-in, and convince them your initiative is a high enough priority to proceed. If you encounter difficulty meeting decision makers, take your idea to someone who may influence them. If they're supportive, they may assist you with meeting decision makers and gaining approval. In your presentation to decision makers, clearly describe your proposal, its benefits, resource requirements, and the decisions or support needed for implementation. To get action on your initiative ahead of other good ideas, establish a sense of urgency. Explain why they should implement your initiative in the near future and the negative consequences of delaying action.

11. **Test Your Initiative:** One effective way to reduce concerns about potential risks and further evolve your initiative is to pilot test it in a limited environment, in a short timeframe or just one part of the organization. This gives you an opportunity to assess the results and make improvements before expanding implementation. It also allows you to tell naysayers, "This is only a pilot test; we can test the concept using limited resources. If it doesn't work, we can walk away from it without any negative impact." You can learn a lot during a pilot test. The lessons learned will provide information for potential improvements and unanticipated opportunities for further benefits. This effective strategy can prove there's significant benefit to pursue your initiative and reduce risk concerns. It can also help with internal politics as you build support working with stakeholders to implement the pilot test.

12. **Assertive Strategies:** These are for the brave at heart! On occasion, you may feel the need to be more aggressive in your approach if you know what you propose is good for your organization and will achieve positive outcomes. You might try these more assertive strategies, but beware, not all organizational cultures (or supervisors!) will support these strategies and may look upon them negatively with potential consequences for you personally. Other organizations may applaud you for finding ways to create an effective path through the bureaucracy. These strategies are most often used when parts of the organization perceive the risks of your initiative as too high and when dealing with internal politics that can't be resolved by the previously mentioned strategies.

   a. **"Unless Otherwise Directed":** Military members often use this strategy, particularly in time-sensitive and mission critical situations, when negative consequences or missed opportunities will occur if you fail to act. You inform superiors of the situation and your intended course of action stating, "Unless otherwise directed, I intend to—" The benefit of this strategy is you inform management of the situation, your assessment, and your intended actions. They must take positive action to intervene if they do not want you to take the recommended action. This strategy can help when dealing with a slow, bureaucratic process and near-term action is needed. Caution: Be careful not to burn bridges with senior managers or key stakeholders.

b. **"Beg Forgiveness versus Ask Permission":** Rear Admiral Grace Hopper of the U.S. Navy, a premier leader in the government's efforts to harness the power of computer technology, coined the phrase, "It's easier to beg forgiveness than to ask permission." Begging forgiveness after an event rather than requesting permission before taking action can be useful when you're confident the results will turn out well and benefit the organization. It's also helpful when you know you'd never get permission to proceed or requesting permission would take too long. You take a risk if the results don't turn out well and you didn't run your initiative through appropriate channels. But if you're confident that you'll achieve significant positive results, you might consider this strategy. Caution: Don't go too far out on a limb. Prepare to mend relationships afterwards if necessary.

c. **"Operating Under the Radar":** Bomber pilots know that if you want to spring a surprise attack, you stay beneath the enemy's radar coverage so you can approach undetected until the last minute, preventing the enemy from mounting an effective defense. The same approach can be useful when attacking the status quo. If they (those entrenched in the status quo and "the way we've always done things") see you coming to change their world, you may be perceived as a threat. They may mount a strong defense and even a counter-offensive before you get a chance to make your case. While I normally encourage transparency and radical inclusion to learn both the best and the worst sides of your initiative, there are circumstances where this strategy can prove effective. Be careful not to posture for short-term gains at the risk of damaging long-term strategic relationships.

c. **"Proceed Until Apprehended":** This is the most radical approach and individuals using this strategy are typically so passionate about their beliefs and initiative, they may risk their career or personal relationships to achieve their goals. On occasion, this may be the only option left and the issue you are dealing with so significant it must be dealt with – gross disrespect or abuse of work colleagues or family members, physical threats, serious breaches of trust and integrity, criminal acts, etc. Seriously consider the consequences before taking this approach. The rewards and risks can be great *and* severe. The risks taken and accomplishments of our founding fathers challenging the British Empire during the Revolutionary War had great outcomes. However, Edward Snowden, the National Security Agency (NSA) worker who provided evidence of the NSA's vast abilities to collect data, also passionately acted on his beliefs with severe personal consequences for himself and national security.

The following table summarizes the twelve strategies and the situations where they may prove helpful.

Table 8.1: Implementation Strategies for Leading from the Middle (1 of 2)

Implementation Strategies	Reasons Ideas Aren't Accepted or Implemented		
	Insufficient Research - Not fully flushed out - Potential technical flaws - Inadequate info for decision makers	**Under/Poorly Conveyed** - Not well understood - Potential supporters unaware of idea - Naysayers exaggerate risks	**Insufficient Benefit** - Can't find a sponsor - Not aligned w/ org. goals - Requires resources - Inadequate opportunity cost
Be the Expert or Engage Experts	X	X	
Bias for Action			X
Sponsor/Champion			
Third Party Assistance	X (SME)	X	
Systems Approach: Understand Big & Little Pictures			X
Build Business Case: Flowchart Process; Info Transparency; Data & Analysis; Performance Metrics		X	X
Network/Partner: Save the Willing First; "Law of Reciprocity"; Critical Mass of Support		X	X
Plan for Failure: Mitigate Negatives; Cause & Effect; Prepare for Wild Success			
Resources: Bootlegging; Share Work/Resources; Phase Work			X
Marketing: Decision Maker Access; Sense of Urgency		X	X
Pilot Test Initiative			X
Assertive Strategies: Unless Otherwise Directed; Forgiveness vs. Permission; Under the Radar; Proceed Until Apprehended			

Table 8.1: Implementation Strategies for Leading from the Middle (2 of 2)

Implementation Strategies	Reasons Ideas Aren't Accepted or Implemented		
	Competing Priorities - One of many good ideas - No urgency - May derail other priorities	**Too Much Risk** - Benefits don't outweigh risks - Organizational - Personal (decision makers or implementers) - Risk-averse culture	**Internal Politics** - Can't access decision makers - Supervisor isn't supportive - Key players threatened - Turf issues - Not invented here
Be the Expert or Engage Experts			
Bias for Action	X		
Sponsor/Champion	X	X	X
Third Party Assistance		X	
Systems Approach: Understand Big & Little Pictures	X	X	X
Build Business Case: Flowchart Process; Info Transparency; Data & Analysis; Performance Metrics	X	X	X
Network/Partner: Save the Willing First; "Law of Reciprocity"; Critical Mass of Support	X		X
Plan for Failure: Mitigate Negatives; Cause & Effect; Prepare for Wild Success		X	
Resources: Bootlegging; Share Work/Resources; Phase Work			
Marketing: Decision Maker Access; Sense of Urgency		X	
Pilot Test Initiative	X	X	X
Assertive Strategies: Unless Otherwise Directed; Forgiveness vs. Permission; Under the Radar; Proceed Until Apprehended		X	X

Applying Strategies for Leading from the Middle

Table 8.1 shows which strategies may be effective against the six showstoppers identified earlier. There's no guarantee any of these strategies will be effective in a specific situation; however, they've been found to contribute toward success and often multiple strategies used together attain positive results. *And* there are often trade-offs between the strategies. For instance, it's nearly always desirable to be an expert, build a strong business case, and take a systems approach. But it may be less critical to network and partner, meet resource requirements, or have an effective marketing strategy if you already have a powerful champion. Every situation is unique. If one combination of strategies isn't working, determine why (which of the showstoppers is kicking your behind?) then try a different strategy.

Table 8.2 shows the strategies applied in the stories of this book. The two most common Leading from the Middle (LFM) strategies are "demonstrating a bias for action" and "becoming an expert," two areas change agents can totally initiate themselves.

Table 8.2:   Real-Life Applied LFM Strategies

Story	Character(s)	Chap.	Strategies Applied
Hurricane Katrina	Rescue Swimmer	1	Be the expert; Bias for action
Hurricane Katrina	Procurement Expert	1	Be the expert; Bias for action
Advising Pentagon Brass	CG Lieutenant	2	Be the expert
Whitewater Rafting & UN General Assembly	Officer as a LT and later as Admiral	2	Be the expert

Story	Character(s)	Chap.	Strategies Applied
Maine Lighthouses	Real Property Specialist	3/7	Bias for action; Network/partner; Systems approach; Forgiveness vs. permission; Under the radar; Champion
Afghanistan GIS Maps	Government Advisor	3	Bias for action; Systems approach; Bootleg resources
Deepwater Horizon Oil Platform Explosion	USCG Commandant	4	Engage experts; Third party assistance; Network/partner; Workload sharing; Sense of urgency
Maritime Counter-terrorism Measures	Coast Guard R&D Center	4	Be the expert; Engage experts; Systems approach; Network/partner; Marketing strategy; Pilot test
Auxiliary Medical Corps	Civilian employee	4	Be the expert; Bias for action; Network/partner
Protecting Medical Convoys in Afghanistan	Military advisor	5	Bias for action; Third party assistance; Business case; Network/partner; Access to decision makers
San Diego Wildfire	Covert Group	5	Bias for action; Engage experts; Systems approach; Bootleg resources; Sense of urgency; Under the radar
Unique Briefing for Secretary of the Air Force	Air Force Officer	5	Be the expert; Bias for action; Systems approach; Business case; Network/partner; Resource sharing; Marketing strategy; Access to decision maker(s)

Story	Character(s)	Chap.	Strategies Applied
Taking on the Pentagon Bureaucracy	Environmental Specialist	6	Be the expert; Bias for action; Third party assistance; Network/partner; Resource sharing; Access to decision maker(s)
Too Much Success	Innovation Council	6	Plan for failure; Marketing strategy; Wild success
CG Innovation Program	Innovation Council	7	Engage experts; Bias for action; Business case; Critical mass of support; Marketing strategy; Champion
CG Information Portal	Mid-grade Officer	9	Be the expert; Bias for action; Network/partner; Bootleg
Heating Failure in CO's Quarters	Facilities Engineer	9	Systems approach; Business case
Life is All About Plan B	Architecture Grads	9	Bias for action; Network/partner; Plan for wild success
QSM Master's Program: Process Improvements	Lieutenant	10	Bias for action; Be the expert; Systems approach; Business case; Resource sharing
Real-time Maritime Domain Awareness	QSM Master's Team	10	Be the expert; Bias for action; Network/partner
Reporting of Suspicious Vessels by Aircraft	Helicopter Pilot & Colleagues	10	Be the expert; Bias for action; Network/partner; Pilot test
Mothballed Helo Flies	Warrant Officer	12	Be the expert; Bias for action; Business case; Bootleg

Strategies

1. **Become *the* expert on your initiative.** Understand its impact, positive and negative, on the workplace. Be able to answer any questions or know where to quickly get the answers.

2. **Develop an effective marketing plan.** Keep in mind you're really marketing two products:

   a. Your change initiative, based on its merits and how it will help your organization; and

   b. You, as a proactive change agent who takes initiative and constantly looks for ways to improve organizational performance.

   Both are important to management and leaders. Even if decision makers don't totally buy into your idea, they may let you proceed with a pilot test of your concept based on your passion, your proven record of success, and your presentation, which shows a reasonable chance of success with minimal risks. *Sell yourself, in addition to your ideas!*

3. **Maximize your initiative's potential return on investment.** Consider direct and indirect benefits and costs. Minimize costs and maximize benefits/opportunities. Build a strong business case.

4. **Address risks directly.** Minimize or mitigate risks to the extent practical, acknowledge remaining legitimate risks, and make a business plan showing why your initiative should proceed, despite any remaining risks, due to the significant benefits it will provide.

5. **Know your competition.** Resources are scarce; learn what other opportunities management may be considering and objectively compare your initiative to the top other opportunities being contemplated. What makes your initiative stand out

from other options? Is your initiative more important, more urgent, more likely to achieve a positive outcome? Likewise, know the people and offices impacted positively or negatively by your initiative. What are their issues, and how can you address their concerns and maximize their opportunities?

6. **Know your initiative's strengths and vulnerabilities.** Assess your initiative using the six statements listed below and consider how to strengthen those with low scores. Determine which combination of strategies may be most useful to promote and implement your initiative (refer to Table 8.1).

   a. **Insufficient Research:** "The solution concept is well researched, based on accurate data, sound analysis, and has no major technical flaws." (5 = max)

   b. **Under/Poorly Communicated:** "The solution concept is clearly conveyed, well understood, and communicated to a broad range of potential supporters." (5 = max)

   c. **Insufficient Benefit:** "The solution concept aligns with organizational goals, has a willing sponsor, a plan to provide required resources, and a sense of urgency." (5 = max)

   d. **Competing Priorities:** "The solution concept has a sufficient opportunity cost or mission urgency to be a high priority compared to already planned initiatives and other good ideas. The concept doesn't threaten to derail other higher priority initiatives and doesn't negatively impact *the big picture*." (5 = max)

   e. **Too Much Risk:** "Benefits of the solution concept clearly outweigh risks to the organization, decision makers, and implementers. Identified risks can be mitigated and are acceptable." (5 = max)

   f. **Internal Politics:** "The solution concept has the support of first- and second-line supervisors and has the interest of decision makers. You identified and addressed the concerns and interests of key players to the extent possible. No major or sensitive political issues are negatively impacted." (5 = max)

Summary

I have been impressed with the urgency of doing. Knowing is not enough; we must apply. Being willing is not enough; we must do.
~ Leonardo Da Vinci

This chapter focused on six primary reasons change initiatives are not accepted and twelve implementation strategies. Table 8.1 identifies which implementation strategies may most effectively counteract potential showstoppers.

Next *UP:* Learning from failure: Leveraging setbacks as a foundation for future success.

Chapter Nine

ARGH#! LEARNING FROM FAILURE

Our greatest glory is not in never falling, but in rising
every time we fall. ~ Confucius

Last chapter, we discussed common issues that prevent initiatives from being approved for implementation and twelve strategies to overcome them. Now we'll examine the most common reasons initiatives fail to achieve expectations and the strategies to avoid or mitigate negative impacts. We'll discuss how to understand and leverage failure (e.g., learning in progress) for future success.

Reasons Change Initiatives Fail to Achieve Expectations

In my thirty-five years of experience, I've seen dozens of failures, those initiatives that failed to achieve the expectations of the initiator and decision makers. Often, initiators who haven't done their homework, researching in detail the potential risks, opportunities, and benefits of their initiative, may unintentionally exaggerate the anticipated results. When those benefits aren't achieved people are disappointed. There's an art to *managing expectations*, both our own and decision makers'. The concept of "under-promising and over-delivering" is described by Tom Peters in his book, *In Search of Excellence*. You need to understand the risks and potential benefits of your initiative and ensure your marketing messages (designed to gain key stakeholders' buy-in and support) and your implementation messages (reporting progress and results) are consistent. Change agents can run into difficulty if they exaggerate potential outcomes during marketing, and the results don't meet the expectations they set.

Several other issues can derail change initiatives. The nine most common I've found are:

- Insufficient qualified staff and/or resources
- Insufficient time
- No one accountable for producing and reporting results
- Insufficient stakeholder engagement
- Ineffective feedback system
- Key supporters depart prior to implementation
- Results take too long to achieve
- An unanticipated derailing event occurs
- Expected results aren't achieved

Insufficient staff and/or resources can be nonstarters and potentially fatal issues, delaying or preventing the start of your initiative. One mitigation strategy is to phase your initiative into smaller, executable pieces you can accomplish within the time available with reduced staffing and resources. Another option is to share the workload with others to reduce your initial resource requirements. You must show progress toward achieving the benefits, so develop a measurable outcome that demonstrates progress and your initiative's value.

The Coast Guard Innovation Council used this strategy to support the chief information officer with developing an enterprise-wide information portal he could not get funded and staffed through the formal budget process. The CIO's program manager, a high-energy, creative, and high-performing lieutenant commander, worked closely with the Innovation Council to obtain funding of discrete foundational subprojects she could execute with existing staff over three years until Coast Guard leaders realized the portal's value and supported it in the traditional budget process. The year following its development, the Coast Guard portal was recognized internationally as one of the fifty best organizational portals and the only one within the U.S. government. The Commandant awarded Lieutenant Commander Jan Stevens the annual Coast Guard Innovation Award for her persistent and successful efforts to provide a valuable capability despite the lack of project resources.

Sometimes you gain approval to proceed, but nobody is assigned the responsibility to produce and report results. When nobody works with the innovator and reports results, it's difficult to sustain progress. You can quickly lose momentum and increase risks that the initiative will wither away. I encountered this while planning to assist FEMA with establishing its own Innovation Program. I prepared a presentation for the Deputy FEMA Administrator and arranged for him to attend the Coast Guard's annual Innovation Expo and meet Coast Guard executives. After attending the Innovation Expo, the Deputy Administrator approved formation of a FEMA Innovation Program. However, he didn't assign anyone responsibility for pulling the Innovation Council together. Then the Joplin, Missouri tornado occurred, and major storms hit the Midwest flooding communities in Kentucky and Tennessee. FEMA senior staff were busy for the next several months responding to the disasters and assisting local communities. The crises faced by FEMA created an impediment to innovation. The Innovation Program initiative was no longer a priority, just another one of many good ideas they may implement in the future.

It's critically important to fully engage stakeholders. Build a critical mass of support by saving the willing first. Find those who realize your initiative's benefits and will work with you. Identify early adopters and bring them onto your team. Develop a breadth of support for your initiative, and also depth in each key area of support. You want to sustain support even if a key stakeholder or supporter disappears before complete implementation. I experienced this with a $1.8 million consulting project for a major DHS component. The undersecretary strongly supported the project, but when he suddenly left DHS, no one continued to champion and oversee the project. Despite all the planning, DHS never implemented the project.

Many initiatives go off track slowly at first and then veer more and more off your intended path to success. Unless you implement a good feedback system to measure progress toward your goal, you may not notice you're off track until you need major course changes. Project management teaches the importance of measuring cost, schedule, and performance. While cost and schedule may be relatively easy to measure, performance can be quite challenging. Develop a straightforward feedback system to determine your progress, effectiveness, and customer satisfaction. Keep the system simple and regularly monitor progress.

Sometimes, despite your best efforts, initiatives get bogged down and take a long time to achieve results, often too long in the minds of management. You can create flexibility by building leeway into your timetable to compensate for unexpected delays. Also, manage expectations by delivering what you promise in a timely manner and clearly explain the reasons for delays.

You may encounter a significant "derailing event" or shift in organizational priorities that seriously impact your initiative. Examples include the 9/11 terrorist attacks which immediately changed research priorities at the Coast Guard R&D Center, and the sequestration of federal budgets in 2013, which resulted in federal agencies shifting their budget priorities to ensure they still met primary mission goals. You may have time to predict the worst-case scenario and take mitigating or preventative action. In other cases, you may have no foresight of the derailing event. If this happens, assess how the new situation impacts opportunities for, and threats to, your initiative. Determine whether being resilient, adapting, or withdrawing is the best strategy.

Sometimes, despite your best efforts, your initiative simply doesn't achieve anticipated results. When this happens, analyze why you didn't attain the desired results. Assess whether your initiative still has merit and can be salvaged. Then, pick yourself up, dust yourself off, and commit to either salvaging your initiative or making a difference with your next best idea.

Table 9.1 shows common reasons initiatives fail and mitigation strategies to counter or avoid the causes of failures.

Table 9.1: Reasons Change Initiatives Fail and Mitigation Strategies for Success:

Reasons Initiatives Fail	Negative Impact	Mitigation Strategies
Insufficient Staff or Resources	Delays/prevents start of initiative	Phase your initiative or share the workload with others to reduce initial staffing and resource requirements.
Insufficient Time	Not enough time to show results or achieve potential	Divide your initiative into smaller phases that can be completed within the allotted timeframe. Develop a measurable outcome that demonstrates the initiative's value.
No one Accountable	Your work isn't a priority	Engage leadership to assign an individual or office responsibility for monitoring your initiative's progress.
Insufficient Stake-holder Engagement	Slows project or limits enthusiasm and support	Build a critical mass of support or save the willing first. Find early adopters and get them on board.
Key Supporters Depart Early	Loss of momentum and critical support	Develop a breadth and depth of support for your initiative, at least two deep for key stakeholders.

Reasons Initiatives Fail	Negative Impact	Mitigation Strategies
Ineffective Feedback System	Problems/Hurdles may go unnoticed	Develop a system to measure progress, cost, effectiveness, and customer satisfaction. Look for negative trends/anomalies. Promptly take corrective action.
Results Take Too Long	Momentum is lost, support wanes	Prepare a detailed plan and timetable (allow for unexpected delays). Communicate the plan and manage expectations.
Unanticipated Derailing Event or Consequences	Resource priorities may shift to other needs	Assess how the new situation impacts opportunities for and threats to your initiative. Determine whether being resilient, adapting, or withdrawing is the best strategy.
Expected Results Not Achieved	Perceptions of value decrease, credibility damaged	Analyze and assess why anticipated results were not achieved. Assess whether your initiative still has merit and can be salvaged.

Losing Heat in the Commanding Officer's Quarters

In February 1994, I was the facilities engineer (FE) of the Coast Guard Recruit Training Center at Cape May, New Jersey. I was responsible for ten maintenance, utilities, and fire protection shops. One day, my deputy called me from the commanding officer's (CO) quarters and asked me to come over.

When I arrived, I found my deputy, warrant officer, boiler plant chief, and two petty officers, all crowded into the small furnace room. They all looked frustrated. My warrant officer told me that, for the third time this month, the captain's quarters had lost heat. The chief broke the bad news. "We know the boiler control is the problem, but none of us know how to fix it." When I asked why, he explained that the old heating system was part of the historic CO's quarters. They weren't familiar with the old boiler's control system because training was hard to get since few companies still repaired boilers like this one. I asked, "Why haven't we received training from a company that still works on this boiler?" He replied, "We've tried for three years, but each year it's cut from the budget because it's not a high enough priority."

I informed my supervisor we needed to hire a boiler control expert to make repairs, and that we'd likely encounter the same costly repair again until we received boiler control training. He wasn't happy but understood.

This wasn't the only time a lack of training had been a problem. I talked with my shop supervisors and learned similar situations had occurred several times. Determined to address these problems, I tasked each shop supervisor to list the skills each member of their shop should be able to perform capably when operating at the full journeyman level. Then I asked them to compare those required skills to their people's actual skills and identify knowledge/experience gaps.

At first, my shop supervisors pushed back due to their busy workloads and the slim chance of this initiative making a difference in our training budget. But they humored me and developed their training/experience gap analyses. When completed, the large number of training deficiencies surprised me, and I better understood how it limited our division's performance and my people's professional growth. The total training deficiency for our division equaled nine times our annual training budget! We developed a fully justifiable and defendable three-year training plan, the costs of which were three times higher than usual, and submitted our budget request for the next year.

I took our training plan to our commanding officer. Instead of being thrown out of his office for bringing an audacious and unrealistic training budget, he said, "I like it. It's clear, defendable, and

demonstrates the consequences for not providing the needed training." In fact, he liked it so much, he made four other division officers
go through the same exercise with their divisions. When it was finished, the command's total training budget request came to three times
recent years' training allocations. My shop supervisors wondered what
would happen and hoped for a twenty to twenty-five percent increase
in training funds.

The Command submitted its training budget request and waited.
Finally, we received word that headquarters approved our training
budget at the entire amount requested! And, two members of my team
received funding for boiler control training!

This was an incredible win on many fronts:

- It showed our people management supported frontline employees' needs to resolve negative outcomes.
- My shop supervisors learned the value of performing analysis to
  justify their needs.
- We demonstrated how to turn failure (heating system failures)
  into a major success by asking key questions, finding the problem's root cause, and developing a resolution plan.

Diagnosing and Understanding the Cause of Failure: Root Cause Analysis

Failure is an essential step to learning. If we take a reasonable approach
to solve problems or achieve goals and apply due diligence to address
the issues discussed previously, and we still don't achieve our objective, it's often due to two reasons: 1) we learn information we weren't
previously aware of or didn't take into account; or 2) information we
based our strategy and assumptions on turned out to be incorrect or
incomplete. In either case, learning accurate information about how
and why your initiative fell short is critical to achieve future success.
Dig deep enough in your failure analysis to learn the true factor(s) that

led to failure, not just surface issues or symptoms. Consultants call this *root cause analysis*.

You can do this analysis by following a process called "Asking the five whys." Toyota Motor Corporation used this process developed by Sakichi Toyoda as part of its problem-solving training in their manufacturing methodology. First, ask why you achieved the outcome you ended up with. Usually there's an apparent cause or reason. Then ask, "Why did this cause occur?" The answer typically reveals an underlying cause. Repeat the process by asking why that underlying cause occurred. Continue asking why until no additional insight is discovered. At this point, you've identified the root cause.

I took the "Five Whys" approach with the heating failure in the captain's quarters:

> "**Why** did the heat system fail?" → "Because the boiler failed."
>
> "**Why** did the boiler fail?" → "Because of a boiler control system failure."
>
> "**Why** can't we fix the boiler control?" → "Because we haven't been trained on this old system."
>
> "**Why** haven't our people received training?" → "Because the command turned down our training requests."
>
> "**Why** weren't requests approved?" → "It wasn't a high enough priority to compete for limited training funds."

Bingo! The "root cause" was found—a lack of training due to a limited budget. Often, getting answers to "why?" questions is more complex and may include collecting data and detailed analysis. But this simple story demonstrates how to perform a failure analysis to determine the root cause.

Predicting Failure Modes: Cause and Effect Diagrams

Rather than waiting for failure and performing an analysis afterwards, wouldn't it be better to predict the most likely failure modes and take preventative actions? In the 1960s, Japanese quality expert, Kaoru Ishikawa, developed the Ishikawa diagram, commonly referred to as a "cause and effect" diagram. While there are other, more sophisticated tools, I often prefer this one because it's simple to understand, it's easy to apply, and you can gain productive insights quickly.

The diagram shows what causes may lead to a negative effect/impact or failure of your initiative. Causes typically fall into six major headings:

1. **Equipment:** computers, machines, etc. needed to perform the task/process
2. **Processes:** methods and procedures used
3. **People:** those involved with the process
4. **Materials:** raw products and supplies needed for the task or process
5. **Environment:** location, climate, temperature, or culture of an organization
6. **Management:** provision of resources, policies, timing, training, etc.

The primary causes are listed off the main headings and secondary causes branch off of primary causes such as unqualified personnel, a lack of training, or installation of new equipment for which training was not yet provided. Figure 9.1 shows a cause and effect diagram for our heating system failure story with the most significant contributing factors in *italics*.

Figure 9.1: Commanding Officer's Quarters Heating System Failure Cause and Effect Diagram

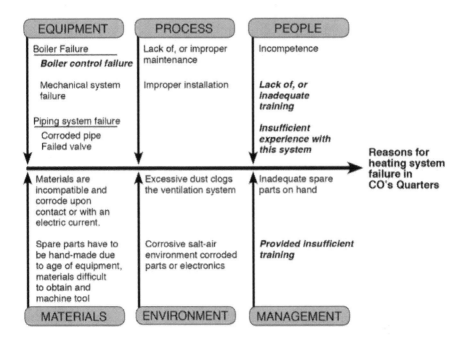

 Strategies

1. **Manage Expectations.** It's always better to under-promise and over-deliver than to over-promise or under-deliver. Be careful what comments you make regarding the expected outcomes of your initiative. Balance the need to market your initiative to gain support with the need to deliver reasonable results to sustain support from key leaders.

2. **Understand the most common reasons for failure.** Consider preparing a cause and effect diagram to determine potential failure modes. Determine which may be most applicable to your initiative and take proactive, preventative action.

3. **If your initiative falls short of expectations, learn why!** Perform a root cause analysis to determine the reasons. Ask the "five whys" to determine the underlying cause of failure. Employ strategies to minimize or mitigate negative impacts.

4. **Get back in the game**! Learn from failure. Pick yourself up, dust yourself off, and get back to work. Either incorporate what you learned to improve your initiative or work on your next best idea.

Summary

> *Never give up, for that is just the place and time that the tide will turn. ~ Harriet Beecher Stowe*

This chapter focused on learning from failure and the nine primary reasons change initiatives fail to achieve expectations. It includes mitigation strategies to avoid potential negative impacts and ways to enhance your change initiative efforts. It also presents useful tools to determine the root cause of failures and to predict possible failure modes so you can take preventative actions.

The below story provides a different application outside of the Coast Guard, military, or first responders that demonstrates the capability of anyone (even unemployed, new college graduates) to apply these principles.

When our oldest son, Matthew, graduated with a degree in architecture, he found it difficult to obtain a full-time architecture position due to the economic slowdown. New graduates competed with experienced architects who had been laid off. He and his classmates excitedly looked forward to using their skills to design new buildings, but they became discouraged by the lack of available positions. Their dreams and career goals were not working out as planned.

While in Tennessee consulting for FEMA, I came across a really neat coffee mug that fit Matthew's situation; it read, *"Life is all about how you handle Plan B."* And on the rim, in small print, it read, *"Plan B..., the true test of character."* He loved it and it became his favorite mug.

While they applied for job after job trying to find full-time employment as architects, Matthew and three buddies – Ryan, Aric, and Mark – formed a group to keep their design skills sharp. They named their group, "Toasting Design," and started entering design competitions. Matthew integrated his college experiences (studies, projects, architectural tours in eight countries and internships) with his friends' experiences into design concepts and projects. He and his roommate, Ryan, leveraged their college course design of a high-rise building in Seoul, South Korea for an international design competition and made the short-list of top designs out of 400 entries! They didn't always have success though, such as their entry into the National "Zombie Safe-House" design competition. But they kept their skills sharp and later, *Toasting Design* won second place in a national affordable housing design competition, winning $700! As they began to have success, they added good material to their resumes.

Eventually Matthew and many of his friends found full-time architecture positions. Matthew followed his passion by 'handling Plan B (and C and D),' never giving up on his goal.

Next *UP:* Tape Measure Your Success/Results: Measuring and Proving Your Progress and Impact

Chapter Ten

Measuring Progress and Impact

I was taught that the way of progress is neither swift nor easy. ~ Dr. Marie Curie

The last two chapters discussed implementation strategies, learning from setbacks, and persevering to achieve your goals. Now we'll discuss how to prove your initiative's value by measuring implementation progress and impact. While *proving* your initiative's value you may discover how to *improve* it by making it more effective or efficient. Likewise, you may discover spin-off or follow-on opportunities enabling you to build upon your initial success. This chapter discusses what is essential to measure to prove progress and impact; the importance of developing an effective feedback system; transforming lessons learned into initiative improvements; developing and expanding your credibility; and leveraging your initiative's success as a foundation for future initiatives.

Partnering with Academia to Improve Organizational Performance

In 2002, I was the chief of quality and management effectiveness responsible for the Coast Guard's Quality Program including twenty-three quality performance consultants (QPCs) who enhanced performance through process improvements. That fall, our Boston QPC,

Lieutenant Lil Maizer, excitedly told me about her Quality Systems Management (QSM) master's program that had terrific promise to improve Coast Guard performance through experiential learning.

A small school on Cape Cod, the National Graduate School (NGS) took a unique approach, combining classroom instruction with practical experience by integrating twelve courses in best business practices with a process improvement team project. To graduate, students had to pass their courses and deliver process improvement project results showing a positive return on investment to their organization, including the cost of tuition! Lil needed to be part of a project team, so she asked other Coasties to consider the program. Twenty-seven Coast Guard personnel (active duty, reservists, and civilians) joined her from Portland, Maine to Cape Cod, Massachusetts.

The Coasties formed seven teams whose projects ranged from reducing costs for replacing buoys after major storms and minimizing Coast Guard cutter maintenance overhaul times, to improving effectiveness of air patrols to detect illegal fishing vessels and streamlining administrative procedures. The school taught students to convert process improvement results, new capabilities, direct savings (funds, personnel, equipment), and reduced process cycle time into a common measure (dollars). The Coast Guard projects' value was estimated at $7.1 million, which was a 17.5-to-1 return on investment (ROI)!

NGS conducted programs at a few sites across the nation, and we explored how to leverage this program more effectively by taking a systems approach to improving Coast Guard processes. Danny Prosser, my NGS liaison, coordinated with Lil to determine how the program could best improve Coast Guard performance. We identified major commands that impacted a significant portion of the Coast Guard budget and strategized about which sites would be most important.

We met with the President of NGS and, within a year, expanded the program to ten sites including headquarters, regional commands, centers for aviation, finance, ship building and repairs, pay and personnel, and logistics! Lil Maizer was awarded one of the first Innovation

Awards at the 2003 Innovation Expo and, from 2003 through 2010, seven hundred Coast Guard employees earned QSM master's degrees and implemented process improvement projects valued by Coast Guard senior champions at $500 million, a 47-to-1 return on the program's tuition costs! The most valuable outcome, however, was developing seven hundred effective change agents who knew how to introduce new and improved processes to significantly enhance organizational performance.

Identifying and Reporting Suspicious Vessels by Aircraft: Failure, then Success!

After the 9/11/2001 terrorist attacks, it became apparent that the process Coast Guard air patrols used to identify vessels that were suspected of fishing illegally; transporting illegal immigrants, narcotics, or terrorists; or other unlawful acts, was woefully inadequate. Aircraft from Air Station Cape Cod (ASCC) conduct a large number of patrols to identify and report vessels operating illegally in closed fishing areas off the New England coast. During a typical four-hour fisheries patrol, aircraft overfly vessels while a crewman attempts to write down vessel names, home ports, and registration numbers in a vibrating aircraft subject to frequent wind gusts. After the patrol, a crew member would take the handwritten data, load it into the Marine Information for Safety and Law Enforcement (MISLE) database, and match it to "lookout lists" to determine if any sighted vessels had violations.

This data entry process could take two hours and, as a result, crews often only reported the most relevant vessel sightings instead of all the vessels sighted to reduce the burden of entering data into the system. In addition, ten to fifteen percent of the data was illegible or couldn't be used due to transcription errors. Once the crewman loaded information into MISLE, the system integrated it into the Common Operating Picture, or COP, that displays locations of suspect vessels and Coast Guard assets that could intercept them. Occasionally, aircrews unknowingly spotted a vessel on a law enforcement lookout list and didn't realize it until after the patrol was over due to the complex process of checking each vessel through several lookout lists. Vessels with outstanding law enforcement violations were rarely apprehended. If an aircraft spotted and identified a possible suspect vessel, say midway in a four-hour patrol, the aircraft would have to land, then enter the information into MISLE, and post the vessel's position in the COP. By the time all this was accomplished, four hours could have passed. Even a slow fishing boat could travel fifty miles during that time making it nearly impossible for a Coast Guard cutter to find and apprehend the vessel.

A group of Coast Guard aviators at Air Station Cape Cod in the QSM master's degree program tackled the challenge of improving the process to identify and report vessels at sea. They teamed with key personnel at the Operations Systems Center (OSC) at Martinsburg, West Virginia, intimately familiar with the MISLE database and the COP. To ensure OSC programmers understood the situation and challenge, Cape Cod aviators invited them to fly on a few fisheries patrols. Together, they developed the idea of downloading relevant portions of MISLE (a database of 160,000 vessels) onto handheld Personal Digital Assistant (PDA) devices that could be taken on aircraft during patrols. By typing vessel sighting information into the PDA, the illegibility issue would disappear. By just typing the first letters of a vessel's name and home port, a menu of vessels in the MISLE database would pop up on the PDA screen and the crewman could select the one corresponding to the sighted vessel. This would save time, improve accuracy, and, through an automatic 'lookout alert,' allow the aircrew to know immediately of vessels on any lookout list. After the patrol, sighting data could be downloaded into MISLE simply by pressing a button.

The team created a business case and applied for ten thousand dollars from the Coast Guard Innovation Council (IC) for prototype PDA devices and OSC programming design time. The IC approved their request, OSC completed the programming, the PDAs were ordered and received, and the team prepared to pilot test their initiative!

Feedback from operational aircrews was absolutely critical to determine required capabilities, how the devices performed, and what to improve.

The pilot test was less than successful because the aircrew experienced difficulty typing on the small PDA keyboard while in flight, given the plane's vibration and the random wind gusts.

Undeterred, the team built upon what they learned to develop *Plan B*, a more expensive, but shock- and vibration-resistant tablet personal computer (PC) with a larger keyboard to better enable typing while airborne. They received additional IC funding after explaining what they learned and describing the impact their project could have.

This time, the pilot test succeeded, and the Air Station implemented use of preprogrammed shock-resistant tablet PCs as part of their standard operating procedures. In addition to improved data accuracy and timesaving features, another unanticipated benefit was found. Because there was no time-consuming post-flight MISLE data entry, and aircrew members could easily enter vessel sighting data while in flight, aircrews identified nearly all vessels sighted, not just suspicious vessels. The new process resulted in Air Station Cape Cod increasing its vessel sightings by five hundred percent. During the first year, Air Station Cape Cod recorded more vessel sightings than all other CG air stations combined. Additional vessel sightings not only increased maritime domain awareness but had a positive impact on other missions. In one case, Coast Guard personnel used sighting data to locate a vessel reported overdue on a transatlantic voyage, saving search and rescue resources. Air Station Cape Cod demonstrated an annual savings of $1.7 million through error reduction and data entry savings, and the ASCC/OSC team received the 2003 Coast Guard Innovation Award for Operations.

Real-Time Maritime Domain Awareness: The Rest of the Story!

Due to Air Station Cape Cod's success with tablet PCs, other air stations became interested. The Office of Aviation bought two tablet PCs for each air station for further testing. Despite the initial success, it could still take two hours to report vessel sightings if spotted mid-patrol. For some Coast Guard missions, most notably interdiction of 'go-fast' boats carrying cocaine, or terrorists threatening U.S. ports, this wasn't timely enough. A second QSM master's team at headquarters built upon Air Station Cape Cod's success to provide near real-time identification of suspicious vessels and COP updates while patrol aircraft were still airborne. The team worked with OSC Martinsburg personnel again and the Aircraft Repair and Supply Center (AR&SC) at Elizabeth City, North Carolina (now the Aviation Logistics Center) to tackle this tough challenge. They also conferred with the Air Station Cape Cod team, particularly Lieutenant Chris Kluckhuhn, a helicopter pilot, who organized and coordinated the initiative there.

After much research, discussion, and partnering with other federal law enforcement agencies and Department of Defense (DOD) military services, the team developed a plan that would allow near real-time transmission of vessel sighting data. Data would be transmitted from a new antenna mounted on the aircraft, uploaded to a DOD satellite system while in flight, and then forwarded to OSC Martinsburg where information would be immediately integrated into the COP for Maritime Domain Awareness. The team encountered several challenges from data protection/encryption issues and information transfer while in flight, to gaining approval to mount an additional antenna on Coast Guard aircraft.

The pilot test was a great success, with vessel sighting data being transmitted, received, and plotted on the COP in less than two minutes, resulting in actionable intelligence for nearly all Coast Guard missions, including high-speed interception of drug cartel 'go-fast' boats or terrorists in maritime ports.

The Coast Guard executive responsible for Maritime Domain Awareness was delightedly stunned by the results the team achieved. He couldn't believe such a small team who weren't systems engineers could solve this complex problem and implement a successful pilot test within such a short timeframe. He estimated the initiative's value at $140 million, which he thought would require the services of the nation's largest defense contractors.

Fast-forward to August 2005. Hurricane Katrina hit southern Mississippi and Louisiana. In New Orleans, the levees breached, flooding the city. I was working with a multi-agency team coordinated by DHS' Office of Information Sharing and Collaboration. We spoke with the chief of logistics for the Joint Field Office (JFO) contingent for Katrina in New Orleans. Communications are down nearly everywhere as emergency generators run out of fuel. The JFO contingent at New Orleans needed to conduct damage assessments quickly to prioritize recovery activities. The logistics chief was desperate for real-time information to ensure damage assessment teams could expedite assistance to where it's most needed. In a conference call I mentioned the tablet PC capability, updated with GPS location devices linked with cameras to transmit live photos and streaming video. Chris Kluckhuhn had also made modifications by adding metropolitan hospital data including available beds for patients and pictures of rooftop helicopter landing zones. The logistics chief said he needed that capability as soon as possible. I called Chris and told him to start generating maps and emergency responder data for New Orleans. After briefing DHS officials, we headed to New Orleans.

Chris, working with a small team, demonstrated the capabilities to other federal agencies including the National Geospatial Intelligence Agency (NGA), Army Corps of Engineers, and the National Oceanic and Atmospheric Administration (NOAA). He showed the use of tablet PCs with camera-interfaces in flights, which impressed local officials. On our fourth day in New Orleans, Rear Admiral Larry Hereth from Coast Guard headquarters visited the New Orleans command center with President Bush. Admiral Hereth informed me the President just designated him as the Principal Federal Official (PFO) for Hurricane Rita heading toward Texas and Louisiana. Our demonstration impressed the admiral and he asked how quickly we could join his new joint field office in Austin, Texas. We joined the admiral forty-eight hours later and prepared to provide near real-time situational awareness to assess damage from Hurricane Rita.

The best time to test a new system's capability isn't in the midst of an emergency. It was chaotic, and we couldn't conduct several tests. But the opportunities to gain *feedback* from operational personnel were incredible as they asked for additional capabilities that wouldn't occur in a normal testing environment. Chris tracked and prioritized requests for the additional features and incorporated what he and the team could on the fly. JFO personnel greatly appreciated the capability provided by the tablet PCs. But what we learned about integrating the most essential capabilities into field operations during an emergency proved priceless and provided opportunities for further improvements.

A few years later, after I'd retired from the Coast Guard, I received an excited call from Chris. He was working the Deepwater Horizon oil spill catastrophe. He said, "Captain, remember the real-time situational awareness capability we pilot tested during Hurricanes Katrina and Rita? Well, I significantly improved the capabilities based on what we learned. Now I'm overflying the Gulf of Mexico near the Deepwater Horizon drilling platform locating oil patches and transmitting live video and GPS coordinates of spills directly to command centers and oil-skimming vessels that proceed to the sites to clean up the oil!" Chris fully implemented our plan to provide real-time situational awareness for disaster assessment and response capability and used it operationally.

Chris and his team developed and operationally implemented an extremely valuable initiative, not just for the Coast Guard, but also for FEMA and other agencies by taking four actions:

1. Measuring their progress and proving headway toward achieving their goal.

2. Measuring impact to prove their initiative's value.

3. Establishing a feedback process to learn what works, what doesn't work, and what's needed.

4. Building upon initial success to achieve success at the next level.

Measuring Progress

What to Measure. Project management teaches us to measure three components to make sure projects stay on track: cost, schedule, and performance. If you keep costs within budget, meet anticipated schedules, and provide a product, capability, or service that meets or exceeds performance criteria, your project will be successful. The same is true of change initiatives.

How to Measure Progress. So how do you measure progress on cost, schedule, and performance? As you plan your change initiative, you must determine expected resource commitments (costs), an implementation schedule, and expectations for results (performance). The following steps can assist you in determining your initiative's expected cost, schedule, and performance. These establish standards against which you can measure actual cost, schedule, and performance to determine progress.

1. Identify the required activities.
2. Determine activity sequencing. Consider whether any activities can be done in parallel.
3. Layout the activities on a timeline.
4. Develop anticipated standards for costs, schedule, and performance at key milestones for your initiative. Allow flexibility for unexpected delays, equipment failures, and minor setbacks.
5. Develop a feedback and progress action plan and share it with stakeholders as appropriate.
   a. Determine how you will track expenses, schedule progress, and performance/quality for comparison against your standards.

b. Determine a regular reporting period to ensure progress is made as expected, and that unexpected delays, cost overruns, or performance/quality issues are identified early.

6. Make process adjustments based upon what you learn during the pilot or implementation phase and continue to obtain feedback for continuous improvement.

Measuring Impact

What to Measure. Change initiatives are typically designed to produce one or more of three benefits:

1. Direct savings
2. Value of a new or enhanced capability
3. Reduction of process cycle time and process improvement

How to Measure Impact. What's a good way to measure your initiative's impact?

1. **Direct Savings:** These are hard savings that can be used elsewhere and include reduced equipment costs, reduced direct maintenance contract costs, fewer materials needed, and less direct labor.

2. **Value of a New or Enhanced Capability:** This can be estimated by the difference between how much it would cost others to develop the capability within the required timeframe and the proposed initiative's cost. Don't forget to include the value of intangible qualities, such as the ability to *safely* transfer hazardous chemicals, the capability to seal the Deepwater Horizon pipeline on the ocean floor in a *timely* manner to avoid hundreds of thousands of additional barrels of oil pouring into the Gulf of Mexico, and the ability to reorganize an organization in a way that doesn't demoralize employees. Each of these intangible effects has a cost if initiatives aren't executed well.

If procedures aren't performed safely, medical insurance costs will rise significantly, and lawsuits may result. If the pipeline isn't capped quickly, it could lead to a catastrophic environmental impact including the fishing and seafood industries. If employees become angry, frustrated, or fearful for their jobs, they may leave an organization which will then incur significantly higher hiring, training, and development costs.

3. **Reduction of Process Cycle Time:** Reducing process cycle time creates 'opportunity value' which isn't direct savings, but rather an opportunity to use the time saved to accomplish additional work. Opportunity value can be converted to dollars, the ultimate currency for decision makers. A simple example shows how to determine the opportunity value of your initiative. A process produces 1,000 widgets at a profit of $10,000 per week. If you improve the process to make the same number and quality of widgets in half the time, you can double production capability and increase your profit to $20,000 per week. *Tip:* When reporting anticipated savings or profit, extend the timeframe to one year since that's the timeframe budget personnel use. In this case, the additional profit, or 'opportunity value,' would be $10,000 x 52 weeks or $520,000 per year. This information provides decision makers the impact of your initiative and options when considering the annual budget.

Feedback and Continuous Improvement

Effective feedback from key stakeholders, operational personnel, and frontline personnel is crucial to identifying issues early and improving your initiative's potential to become a "best practice." This is especially important during your pilot test period as you want to eliminate glitches prior to full-scale implementation. Air Station Cape Cod's team clearly realized the importance of feedback when inviting OSC Martinsburg programmers to observe their initial PDA prototype's performance while in flight. By flying on missions and interviewing aircrew about the utility of their device and software, they quickly realized the need for improvements, the most important being a larger keyboard to enable typing while airborne.

The key to success is to act on feedback as effectively and quickly as possible. Doing so shows stakeholders you listened to them and gives you another chance to test the "improved version," thus gaining both credibility and building future support once you get it right.

On rare occasions, you may need to pilot test your initiative before it's fully ready to take advantage of an incredible opportunity for a field test. This occurred when Chris and I deployed for Hurricanes Katrina and Rita. Although Chris hadn't yet perfected the "ruggedized" tablet PC's and situational awareness software, others (federal, state, and local emergency responders) could clearly see their potential and thought of ingenious potential applications. "If it could have this capability, we could then. . . " "Can you include an option to do 'x?'" "Can you configure it to link up with partner organizations' data such as metropolitan firefighters, police, FEMA, or DOD?" and many more. While it was difficult to make adjustments in the field during hurricane response operations, Chris documented the suggested applications and continued to improve the initiative. By the time the Deepwater Horizon oil spill occurred, he had a fully operational capability that, while airborne, transmitted video displays showing the time and position of oil spills to the surface skimming vessels.

Building on Success

So how can you leverage your success to develop future initiatives? First, recognize the value *you* bring to the organization, not just having a good idea, but gaining support for your idea, partnering and collaborating with others, convincing the organization to provide resources, testing your concept, implementing your idea, and measuring and proving its value. Whether the initiative saves your work unit $5,000 a year, or the Coast Guard $140 million, people who can take a good idea from conception to implementation are priceless. Once you prove you can be successful, you gain credibility with peers and decision makers.

Once you earn credibility, more doors open to you. You'll be invited to problem-solving or strategy meetings, asked your opinion as a subject matter expert, or be asked to join cross-functional teams to overcome significant challenges. You also have an opportunity to meet like-minded people, other change agents who may stimulate your thinking and provide capabilities and expertise that may aid current or future initiatives. You can plant the "seeds" of ideas you would ultimately like to pursue, and see if colleagues have helpful ideas, or know others who might assist you. All the while, you continue building your personal and professional network, creating a broader foundation for launching future initiatives.

Chris Kluckhuhn and the Air Station Cape Cod team won the Coast Guard's Innovation Award, and Chris served as a subject matter expert for the HQ/OSC/AR&SC team to provide real-time situational awareness from Coast Guard aircraft. Highly regarded as a Coast Guard innovator, Chris earned credibility, which opened doors for him with decision makers. This resulted in Chris getting a rare opportunity to speak about innovation to all the Coast Guard's admirals and civilian executives at a breakfast meeting at the Innovation Expo. Chris described the challenges faced by Coast Guard innovators and how executives' responses (in briefings, policy statements, and resource decisions) often gave innovators mixed signals that could lead to confusion and misinterpretation. Sometimes executives encouraged innovation, but the bureaucracy took so long to make decisions that they lost opportunities. Chris had the courage to speak truth to power about significant concerns faced, not only by himself, but many others attempting to improve the Coast Guard by leading *from the middle*. He *proved* his concept for providing more timely situational awareness from aircraft patrols, *improved* it with others to provide a real-time situational capability to update the Common Operating Picture, *tested* the concept, *learned of additional valuable applications* during Hurricanes Katrina and Rita, *implemented* it, and showed its value during the Deepwater Horizon oil spill.

But most importantly, Chris, through his passion, energy, operational and technical skills, and innovative nature, built credibility and a reputation with his colleagues and leaders for tackling difficult challenges and developing workable solutions. To adapt a popular television commercial from the 1980s, "When Chris Kluckhuhn spoke about innovation, people listened!" When decision makers supported Chris' initiatives, they often supported the proven innovator *behind* the ideas more than the specific initiative. Chris had built a proven foundation of success from which he launched future initiatives.

 Strategies

The following strategies will assist you with proving, improving, and implementing change initiatives to develop your personal credibility and reputation for success.

1. **Determine and use Performance Metrics: Prove the value!** Measure both the *progress* and *impact* of your initiative.

2. **Develop a Feedback System for continual improvement:** Develop a system that provides information about progress on *cost* and *schedule,* and the impact with regard to your initiative's *performance.* Use feedback to determine what works well and what to improve. Take action to transform lessons learned into initiative improvements.

3. **Document Success:** Regularly record progress and performance to inform decision makers and build your reputation and credibility for producing success.

4. **Identify Who will Sustain the Initiative:** Think beyond the pilot test to full-scale implementation. Who (individuals/offices) will ultimately provide policy guidance, standard operating procedures, and resources to fully implement your initiative? Partner with them for a smooth transition from prototype/pilot test to full implementation.

5. **Leverage Success for Spin-off Improvements/Initiatives:** Look for opportunities to speak about your successful initiative and influence others about future initiatives as possible spin-off improvements. Leverage your initial success to broaden your circle of influence and gain support for your next initiative!

Summary

Nothing in the world can take the place of persistence. Talent will not; nothing is more common than unsuccessful men with talent. Genius will not; unrewarded genius is almost a proverb. Education will not; the world is full of educated derelicts. Persistence and determination alone are omnipotent.
~ Calvin Coolidge

Olympic athletes competing in the javelin throw, shot put, or long jump have efforts measured by a tape measure stretched from the initial throw or leap to where the javelin, shot put, or jumper landed. The tape measure determines the competitor's performance and records the results. This chapter focused on how to "tape measure" your initiative's performance, progress, and impact. It discussed the importance of developing a feedback system to determine progress and the performance resulting from your initiative to not only *prove* but *improve* results. Finally, it described how to leverage your initial success to build credibility and a positive reputation for producing results to help you succeed in future initiatives.

Next UP: Helpful coping and exit strategies if you're working in a hostile or caustic environment.

Chapter Eleven

WORKING IN DEATH VALLEY

Being challenged in life is inevitable, being defeated is
optional. ~ Roger Crawford

While reviewing an outline for this book, my lovely and practical wife, Lisa, made an astute observation. She told me nearly all the stories were about people working in organizations that *support* proactive personnel who take the initiative to make improvements. "What about people working in less than ideal, or even barely tolerable situations? What advice and tools can you provide them to improve their situations, productivity, and happiness?" She was absolutely right, so I added this chapter on helpful strategies for those in a hostile, toxic, or desolate environment.

If you work in an organization with a negative culture and discuss the situation with friends, often their advice may be, "If it's that bad, why don't you just leave?" But life isn't that simple; people tolerate negative environments for many valid reasons including:

- My son/daughter just started college, and I can't risk losing income while paying tuition.

- My spouse or child is seriously ill and despite the difficult work environment, we have an excellent medical plan that covers most expenses.

- My difficult boss retires in five months.
- My 401K will be vested in eight months which is key to my retirement plan.

The examples below describe various organizational environments. This chapter focuses on the top three (more negative) and suggests strategies to consider.

1. **Hostile environment:** Blatant, illegal sexual harassment, age discrimination, or violent threats are part of your day-to-day workplace. You may take legal action, e.g., filing grievances or lawsuits, but be certain you understand the likely outcomes before proceeding as significant career risks may exist.

2. **Emotionally toxic environment:** This type of environment may be due to the anger management issues of a colleague or supervisor, or you're subject to bullying, subtle ongoing threats, and verbal or psychological abuse that falls just short of being illegal.

3. **Results-only work environment:** The organization focuses only on procedures, systems, and outcomes. Employees don't matter. Management doesn't care about your development or welfare as long as you produce results. There's no concern or consideration for staff well-being.

4. **Good work environment:** You have nothing serious to complain about. You receive decent pay, have a good/safe workplace, and decent management, but the organization fails to encourage people to reach their full potential to be exceptional. The environment is tolerable, but falls well short of encouraging and empowering its people to be proactive, take initiative, and assume ownership for the organization's results and ultimate success.

5. **Outstanding environment:** Employees are appreciated, fully engaged, and thrive on challenges:

   a. Catching and celebrating employees doing well, versus pouncing on them for mistakes

   b. Encouraging suggestions and implementing them, not just filing them away

   c. Helping employees find and use their personal strengths on the job

If you're in an organization with a negative environment, ask yourself if the problem is the organization overall (culture, climate) or just one or two key players (the CEO, your supervisor, a colleague). While organizational environment is a key factor in the recruitment, development, and retention of talented personnel, research shows the most common reason people leave organizations is their relationship with their supervisor. Also, honestly consider whether your actions or attitude contribute to your perceptions of a poor workplace environment. If they do, can you adopt a more positive attitude, give your supervisor and colleagues the benefit of the doubt, and make constructive contributions that could begin to change people's opinions about the workplace or even about you?

Changing Fortunes

Sometimes a good situation can change into a difficult work environment. This happened to me after retiring from the Coast Guard. Initially, I worked directly for the director of an organization and actively engaged in major policy meetings and strategic planning sessions. The director respected my opinions and I felt good about my contributions and the assistance I provided our clients, federal agencies.

Later, I worked for a new supervisor below the director. In the following months, the director resigned, and the supervisor I worked for showed little appreciation for the expertise I brought to the job. As I observed my supervisor's management style, I realized the supervisor wasn't acting this way only toward me. My supervisor was also like this with a former senior Navy medical officer with extensive experience responding to international natural disasters, and a colleague with two decades of experience managing environmental disaster cleanups. The supervisor focused on producing academic reports—with the primary goal of surviving the scrutiny of other research institutions—rather than identifying shortcomings and opportunities to implement solutions to improve performance. While the previous director valued and respected my operational perspective and experience, my new leadership team had a more bureaucratic focus. In fact, our supervisor didn't even accompany two of us to meet agency sponsors of major studies. The winds had changed. In reality, the federal agencies we supported benefitted from both operational real-world experience *and* academic rigor.

Over time, it became obvious that management no longer highly valued operational expertise. I entered a doctorate in business administration (DBA) program designed for working professionals to conduct research in an area of my passion: innovation, empowering people, and leadership. While working on my degree, the situation at work deteriorated. On a Sunday, as my Navy friend and I worked to meet nearly impossible deadlines, he shared his frustration that management didn't leverage his skills. He was working as an "expert" in a field he knew little about. He appeared distraught and felt certain he'd be fired.

I worked on eight major tasks one year with only one being for my direct supervisor (we practiced matrix management). For my efforts, I received a less-than-stellar evaluation that included little input from four other managers I'd worked for who were very pleased with my efforts. My supervisor gave me an ultimatum: take a $30,000 pay cut or resign. The organization also laid off my environmental expert friend, even though her efforts led directly to $6 million of work.

I didn't like the way management treated our people. They rarely leveraged people's strengths and limited professional growth opportunities, especially for junior and mid-grade staff. Then there were the short-notice layoffs. Yet, I couldn't just walk away from my job with our oldest son in college and our youngest son battling a serious health issue with significant medical expenses—$250,000 one year. In addition, I'd started my DBA degree program, didn't have a new job to jump to, nor time for an in-depth job hunt. While I didn't feel a deep attachment to our management team and the culture they created, I felt a strong attachment to our clients, their mission, and helping them serve the nation. I reluctantly absorbed the pay cut and focused my discretionary efforts on completing meaningful research in support of my doctoral program, to help others, and do the best job I could for our clients. I remained totally professional while keeping a relatively low profile, and I selectively picked junior and mid-grade staff to mentor and develop.

I graduated with my DBA in the summer of 2011. Earning the degree was a significant achievement, but for several classmates it became a means to an end by opening new doors of opportunity. In my case, it led to a new career teaching leadership, one I'd wanted to enter for a long time but didn't have the experience and sufficient credentials for.

Two months after I graduated, a colleague I highly respected made me aware of a leadership faculty opening at a federal agency. I applied, went through the hiring process, and left my less-than-ideal position. I was finally able to do what I really wanted to do: help develop and positively influence the current and next generation of public sector leaders on issues such as inspiring trust, emotional intelligence, conflict management, effective teamwork, feedback, communications, and management styles.

While preparing to leave my organization, I was careful not to talk negatively about management, my supervisor, or the organization. They had a good mission and a lot of great people really trying to make a difference, and I genuinely cared about several of my co-workers. I was pleasantly surprised at my going-away affair that the new director, both vice-presidents, several managers and forty coworkers showed up, thanked me for my service, and wished me well. I still often meet former coworkers to catch up. I've also served as a reference for several to further their professional careers. I left on good terms.

With the help of colleagues and friends, and support of my family, I transitioned from a difficult work environment to one that allows me to develop, grow, and chase my passions. Even better, I get to assist others in their leadership journeys. I made the transition relatively gracefully without negativity or burning any bridges, while maintaining important relationships.

Whether to Leave or Stay: Exit Strategies and Coping Strategies

When faced with a difficult, hostile, toxic, or even a good work environment, we have two choices. We can either stay or leave. As mentioned earlier, there are several valid reasons people stay in difficult organizational environments. People who choose to leave typically develop an *exit strategy* to give thoughtful consideration to critical matters: when should I leave, where will I work next, do I have enough savings until I start another position, what will I do for medical insurance, etc.? People who choose to stay, whether consciously or subconsciously, develop *coping strategies* by keeping a low profile, avoiding their supervisor or the "hothead" in the office, going to night school to broaden or deepen their professional background, getting cross-training assignments or taking professional development classes to create new opportunities, or just doing the minimum necessary to survive the week. A third option is a hybrid solution: implementing a coping strategy as a temporary measure until they're in a good position to execute their exit strategy.

Experts are divided on whether people should stay or leave when operating in a difficult environment. Some say leave only as a last resort; others say to bail out at the first opportunity. I can't advise you on whether you should stay or leave a difficult environment because each situation and individual is unique. However, if faced with the potential for physical harm, you should take action to resolve the situation or leave as soon as possible. Keep in mind though, it can be economically and emotionally disastrous to leave a job situation without a new job to go to, especially in a tough job market.

In discrimination or sexual harassment cases, you may have limited options if you report inappropriate behavior and no action is taken. In one sexual harassment situation, a coworker was sending several employees pornographic emails. Complaints to the individual sending the emails did no good, and when one of the aggrieved employees complained to her manager, the manager took no action. The bad behavior continued to be tolerated. Her eventual solution was ingenious for both its simplicity and effectiveness. She found a Supreme Court ruling that stated employers had a responsibility to protect employees from offensive email. Knowing her complaints were ineffective, and wishing to maintain anonymity, she came into the office early one morning and posted the Supreme Court ruling on the bulletin board and left a copy on everyone's desk. No one knew who posted the ruling, but a reasonable person might assume upper management sent a message that this inappropriate behavior would not be tolerated. The offensive emails abruptly stopped.

Some say continuing to work in a challenging environment under difficult circumstances can be a "growth" experience as in, "Welcome to the real world!" But it may just be a waste of your time and talents when you could be much happier somewhere else. Most agree you should continue to perform to the best of your ability, if for no other reason than to obtain a good reference for your next position. More importantly though, don't lower your standards due to a bad situation or supervisor or mistreatment by a colleague. Do your best work and keep in mind you have a career or personal goal that extends beyond the current position. Keep your longer-term vision in mind as you move forward.

Some advice to consider if you decide to stay in your organization:

- **Stay fully occupied.** Focus on your position and responsibilities, not the negative climate. Perform at a high level despite the difficult culture. Continue to make valuable contributions. You can have a positive impact and feel good about your efforts.

- **Focus on the good things you do.** In your current position, continue supporting the mission, providing great service to clients, or coaching a colleague. Think about what makes you proud because when you start thinking positively about a situation, negative actions tend to have less impact on you.

- **Make adjustments in your position.** Be more active in the areas you enjoy and do more of what you're really good at.

- **Reduce negativity and make improvements.** Even small things can change the tone within your work group: warmly greet your colleagues, wish them an enjoyable weekend, and compliment them when they do a good job.

- **Manage your own expectations.** If you and your ideas weren't already appreciated, don't expect to be. The organizational climate isn't likely to change significantly.

- **Improve your ability to work with challenging individuals.** Anticipate areas of possible conflict and prepare yourself before entering into difficult conversations.

- **Handle conflicts as they occur.** If you deal with office bullies, avoid arguments, if possible, and don't raise emotional levels by using a loud voice or words and phrases that may trigger a hypersensitive negative response. Bullies thrive on those types of responses. Don't lower your standards to their level.

- **Diffuse tense situations.** If possible, find a diplomatic way to change, end, or exit a difficult or tense conversation quickly. Then leave and stay away until the situation cools down.

- **Don't get frustrated over issues you're powerless to change.** Becoming frustrated over issues you can't change causes stress and uses tremendous energy. This is energy you could use more constructively such as increasing your skills or expanding your professional network. In some cases, you may just have to accept the situation and move on.

- **Spend time with like-minded colleagues.** Sharing thoughts with supportive friends with similar viewpoints can raise your morale. Find time to have coffee or lunch and chuckle at the insanity of your organization. People feel better when they realize they're not alone.

Below are some specific *coping strategies* if you decide to stay in your organization:

- **Transition or transfer to another office:** This option is particularly helpful if you have a difficult supervisor or coworker but are committed to the organization's mission.

- **Stay until a specific date or event:** Plan your exit strategy when you can see the light at the end of the tunnel based upon an upcoming event that changes the situation (a challenging colleague transfers or retires) or gives you freedom to make new choices (your daughter/son completes college or you earn a new degree).

- **Search for opportunities to make a difference:** While you may not be successful changing an organization's culture or negative environment, you still can positively impact individuals and make contributions toward a mission you strongly believe in. Search for personally satisfying opportunities.

- **Keep a low profile:** Accept your current situation and focus on doing your job. Use discretionary efforts for personal or professional growth beyond your current position.

- **Wait out sensitive issues or until difficult characters depart:** Circumstances and people change with time, if you can, hang in there!

- **Work remotely:** Being offsite tends to minimize conflicts and issues. But don't become isolated.

If your situation becomes intolerable and you decide to leave, consider the following advice:

- **Determine what really matters to you and where you can make a difference:** When looking for new opportunities, you can continue activities you're already familiar and experienced with, or you can try something totally new! Don't simply look for a position for a paycheck. Consider the question Jim Collins asked companies while researching his best-selling book *Good to Great*: "Why not be Great?"

- **Find something you enjoy and can excel at:** As researched by best-selling author Marcus Buckingham, we frequently spend too much time trying to overcome weaknesses rather than leveraging our strengths. Imagine a position where you can use your strengths and follow your passions, then research and network to find what opportunities exist.

- **Leverage your personal/professional networks:** Let friends and colleagues know what you're interested in. You never know who your friends know and what may be available. Leaving may not always be your best option, but be prepared if a great opportunity emerges.

- **Timing can be important:** Consider factors that might impact *when* may be the best time to leave. Consider things like after your retirement plan is vested, prior to the next round of layoffs, after your loved one is well, etc.

- **"Do no harm" to yourself or your organization:** Practice the medical profession's motto of *do no harm*. Leave your organization with your head held high as a respected professional. Protect and preserve your reputation. Don't talk badly about your organization, trash your supervisors, or gossip as this can frequently come back to hurt you. People will wonder what you may say about them in the future.

- **Don't burn any bridges:** You don't know what the future holds, and even someone who didn't treat you well may be in a key position to help you in the future.

Below are some specific *exit strategies to consider* if you decide to leave your organization:

- **Seek professional development opportunities:** Take advantage of training and seminars available through your current workplace, professional societies, etc.

- **Expand your personal and professional networks:** Reach out to others in areas of interest, let them know what you're interested in. Expand your network.

- **Update your resume:** Bring your resume up-to-date and tailor it to specific opportunities of interest. Include articles you've written, presentations at professional conferences, professional licenses or certifications earned, and relevant courses taken.

- **Expand your education:** Consider taking courses or entering a degree or certificate program to broaden your credentials, experience, and contacts in your field of interest.

- **Volunteer:** Work in an area of interest to gain experience and expand your network.

- **Join professional societies, organizations:** Increase knowledge and expand your network by meeting new people.

- **Attend professional conferences, meetings:** Gain professional knowledge and expand your network to obtain possible job leads in your area of interest.

During my "Changing Fortunes" story discussed earlier, I used a combination of coping and exit strategies to prepare for a graceful exit from a bad situation and to start a new career I felt passionate about. When it became obvious the environment was unlikely to improve, I considered whether to stay or leave. Although I could have left and found a similar job, it wasn't what I wanted to do long-term, and I would have assumed an economic risk as our oldest son started college. Despite the reduction in pay, I stayed with my organization temporarily, and prepared myself for a career change I'd really enjoy.

The coping and exit strategies I used to transition to a new career and organization included continuing to perform good work for our clients, keeping a low profile, and finding time to mentor and develop selected junior and mid-level professionals. At the same time, I expanded my professional knowledge about innovation, empowerment, and leadership through my research and academic studies while building a new and expanded professional network. I let others know my interest in teaching leadership and, ultimately, an excellent opportunity emerged. I also gave talks and presentations on leading *from the middle* and wrote professional articles, which added to my credentials in leadership development. Once I earned my degree, I more aggressively pursued my job hunt and professional networking. Nearly as important, I didn't talk poorly about my supervisor, and *did no harm* to my organization or my professional reputation. I left on good terms and embraced my new position, teaching leadership.

 Strategies

If you're in a hostile, toxic, or desolate environment, the following strategies may help.

1. **Analyze your situation and your options.** It's easy to say something in the heat of the moment you may regret later. If you've been treated unfairly or aren't appreciated, consider the following:

○ Did a single event, or series of events or situations lead you to feel mistreated, underappreciated, or abused?

○ If a single event, did one individual trigger it and can the issue be addressed and corrective action taken? Are you partially responsible for the situation and is it repairable?

○ If there is a series of events, can you identify a trend, and are they focused on you personally or professionally?

○ If the event(s) focus on you professionally, is there any legitimacy to the issues? What positive actions you can take to improve the situation?

○ If the event(s) focus on you personally, is there discrimination or bullying involved which you might discuss with the human resources department or consider for legal action?

2. **Decide whether you want to stay in the organization, stay temporarily, or leave.** Based on your analysis and understanding of your current situation ask yourself:

○ Can you turn the situation around?

○ Are there likely to be any significant changes in the near future that may positively impact the situation?

○ Is the situation likely to stay the same or get worse?

○ Is the situation tolerable? Do the potential gains of leaving outweigh the risks?

3. **If you decide to stay.** For the short-term or longer, *determine which coping strategies to use*:

○ Transition to another office

○ Stay until a specific date or event and plan your exit strategy if the situation doesn't improve

○ Search for opportunities to make a constructive difference

◦ Keep a low profile. Wait out sensitive issues until the situation is less volatile or until bad characters transfer, retire or leave

◦ Maximize remote work possibilities, but don't become isolated!

◦ Focus on your responsibilities/performance while looking for options to improve the situation

4. **If you decide to leave.** *Make sure you know where you want to go*:

◦ What direction do you want to take? What is the endpoint you want to achieve?

◦ What is the best way to get there?

◦ Who can help?

◦ Is timing important?

5. **Form your exit strategy.** Determine *which exit strategies will help you reach your new destination*:

◦ Seek professional development opportunities

◦ Network professionally

◦ Update your resume

◦ Expand education in your field of interest

◦ Volunteer to work in an area of interest

◦ Join professional societies, organizations, etc.

◦ Attend professional conferences, meetings, etc. in your area of interest

6. **Do no harm**. Protect your personal and professional reputation and that of your organization.

Summary

We must have perseverance and above all confidence in ourselves. We must believe that we are gifted for something and that this thing must be attained.
~ Dr. Marie Curie

This chapter focuses on how to deal with a hostile, negative, or desolate environment. It discusses valid reasons people stay in bad environments and describes *coping strategies* to consider if you choose to stay, as well as *exit strategies* if you plan to leave. Determine the actions you can take to create a more positive future, either within your current organization, or in a new opportunity.

Next *UP*: Call to Action: Make an impact contributing to an energized and engaged environment!

Chapter Twelve

CALL TO ACTION

*Far and away the best prize that life has to offer is
the chance to work hard at work worth doing.*
~ Theodore Roosevelt

A while back I had dinner with a forward-thinking and innovative friend, Kitty Wooley. She'd recently retired after an impressive and impactful career in the federal government. Kitty coached, mentored, and encouraged more public sector employees than I could possibly count. She was excited about my *leading from the middle* concepts and told me an interesting story about someone she knew. We'll call him "Sam."

Sam worked for a very restrictive federal agency, but he was also an "idea guy." He was always coming up with new ideas to improve processes and efficiency within his workplace and agency. Unfortunately, the culture where Sam worked was stuck in the status quo. They wanted to do things the way they'd always been done and didn't see any reason to change. The organizational culture was so rigid that very few of Sam's ideas were implemented. The rest he simply filed away. Sam continued coming up with new ideas to improve processes, mission effectiveness, and customer satisfaction year after year. He'd suggest new ideas, have them shot down, and then file them. Sam appreciated a lot about the work he and his teams accomplished, but there were other things he wanted to do more. So, after nineteen years, he gave up a nearly sure path to becoming a federal executive and left his agency—with a file cabinet full of good, unimplemented ideas.

Sam made a conscious choice to postpone ideas not consistent with his agency's culture, but he implemented some of his best ideas *outside of work* such as forming a collective of like-minded federal employees who wanted to improve the federal government. This group partnered with Young Government Leaders and other organizations to offer opportunities for people with good ideas to be heard. They created FedPitch, a grassroots initiative providing citizens opportunities to present their good ideas to improve the federal government. They took an innovative approach, asking federal employees to "Imagine you're in charge and have all the time, talent and money in the world. What would you do to effect positive change in your department? Your agency? Your government?" Finalists with the best ideas teamed with speechwriters who helped them effectively communicate their ideas before a live audience and judges' panel during Public Service Recognition Week on the National Mall in Washington, DC.

Sam later became the director of leadership development for the Senior Executive Association. Sam found that to chase his vision of influencing and implementing positive change and encouraging others to do so, he had to *take his best ideas and work outside the organization* and eventually leave. The sad thing is cultures that force people to do their best work outside their workplace lose out on the benefits they could derive from implementation in-house.

Let's contrast Sam's story and the legacy he left (a filing cabinet full of unexplored ideas) with the results of the *Unauthorized Progress* stories:

- Hurricane Katrina rescue swimmer who bought fire axes at a hardware store at midnight to save families trapped in their attics by rising waters (Chapter One)

- Procurement specialist who expedited orders during Hurricane Katrina so first responders could save lives and property (Chapter One)
- Real property specialist who arranged the transfer of twenty-eight Coast Guard lighthouses to Maine communities and non-profit organizations to better preserve the lighthouses and save taxpayers millions of dollars (Chapter Three)
- Sixty-something CG Auxiliarist who initiated a CG Auxiliary Medical Corps comprised of four hundred volunteers providing medical and dental exams for Coast Guard reservists deploying to the Middle East (Chapter Four)
- Air Force officer who convinced the Secretary of the Air Force that a new wartime capability could also be a valuable tool to save lives during natural disasters (Chapter Five)
- Environmental specialist who challenged Pentagon bureaucracy to create a win-win situation by arranging for DOD divers to assist the Coast Guard in cleaning up hundreds of coastal environmental sites (Chapter Six)
- Small team of mid-level Coast Guard aviators, logistics experts, and software specialists who improved maritime domain awareness by reducing reporting times for suspect vessels from over four hours to two minutes, valued at $140 million (Chapter Nine)
- Lieutenant whose efforts led to her championing a program that resulted in seven hundred Coast Guard employees earning master's degrees in Quality Systems Management and leading to process improvements valued at $500 million (Chapter Ten)

As demonstrated by the actions of those mentioned above, *Unauthorized Progress* is intended to encourage and inspire leaders at *all* levels, regardless of position, to be proactive and take initiative to improve their organizations and accomplish their goals. This book provides strategies you can apply to implement constructive change and effectively *lead from the middle*. In the process, you'll become more fulfilled and lead a personally more energized, engaged, and rewarding life.

Creative Solution to Replace Crashed Helicopter

On December 8, 2004, an MH-60 helicopter assigned to Coast Guard Air Station Kodiak, Alaska crashed during search and rescue operations near Unalaska Island. Its loss created a serious challenge as it was one of forty-two unique helicopters built for the Coast Guard by Sikorsky Aircraft during the early 1990s. The original production line for these helicopters had been retooled and replacement options were limited. Although the Coast Guard could procure a one-of-a-kind S-70B aircraft for $27 million, it would have a significantly different structural configuration than the rest of the Coast Guard's helicopters, making depot and unit level maintenance more complex and expensive. Delivery time for a new S-70B aircraft was expected to take three years. The excessive procurement and sustainment costs combined with the extensive production lead time made this option unattractive.

After completing a thorough engineering analysis, Chief Warrant Officer Montgomery Everson, assigned to the Coast Guard's Aviation Logistics Center, determined that a retired Navy SH-60F could be converted into the Coast Guard's unique MH-60T configuration at a substantially lower cost than a new procurement. Working closely with the original equipment manufacturer and Naval Air Systems Command, Chief Warrant Officer Everson developed a procedure to modify significant portions of the SH-60F to produce a replacement aircraft indistinguishable from any other Coast Guard MH-60 aircraft for $15 million, saving over $12 million compared to procuring a new aircraft. His industrial process was prototyped to create a replacement aircraft, which began flying operationally in September 2009. The new industrial process reduced delivery time by eighteen months. Furthermore, the Aviation Logistics Center used Chief Warrant Officer Emerson's process to convert a second Navy helicopter hull into a spare Coast Guard MH-60 hull.

What About You?

Leading change is hard. Some days you may think, "This is difficult, much harder than I thought . . . and it's taking much longer than it should. Is it worth it?" *Unauthorized Progress* provides strategies to help you maximize your opportunities to make a difference in your organization and to have a positive impact while minimizing risks. So, what holds you back? Why do people hesitate to stretch to their potential? Some reasons people with great ideas don't pursue them include:

- **Fear of failure:** What are the *real* consequences? They may be more imagined than real. Consider any failure as a learning opportunity to get better. Instead of thinking "What happens if I fail?" turn this upside down and consider "What happens if I succeed?"

- **Concern of what the experts will say:** Those closest to the process or customer often know more than so-called experts who aren't as familiar with your process, culture, and customers. Become *the* expert on your initiative so you can address any questions.

- **Intimidated by colleagues or supervisor:** Build a coalition of support that overwhelms naysayers.

- **Working in a punitive culture:** Review the coping and exit strategies in Chapter Eleven.

- **Fear of speaking up:** Ask "What if?" and "Why not?" Work to build confidence in this area and/or find a colleague who's willing to be an effective spokesperson for your ideas.

- **Poor presentation skills:** Build and leverage a great team around your initiative. Use the talents of the team to present your ideas. Improve your skills and confidence.

- **Fear of conflict:** Determine which battles are worth fighting and prepare for them with data, stakeholder support, and a solid business plan that clearly demonstrates your initiative's value.
- **Lack of resources:** Phase your initiative or share resources with another office.

What are the rewards of being successful? They may not be tangible, not monetary or an immediate promotion. They may simply be self-satisfaction and acknowledgement from your supervisors and peers that your idea made things better for your co-workers, your customers, and your organization. There may also be a willingness, perhaps even eagerness, that others may develop to hear your next great idea, one they may want to be a part of. Being proactive, taking initiative and *leading from the middle* is a way to live a more rewarding life, where you're actively engaged and energized and looking forward to each day as an opportunity to make a positive contribution. You're making a difference in ways that matter to you, your colleagues, and your organization.

 Strategies

The concepts and strategies presented in *Unauthorized Progress* can be consolidated into three overarching strategies to identify and effectively act on your good ideas.

1. **Ideation and Evaluation:** (Chapters One through Four) If you already have an initiative idea, go to step two
   ○ Use the strategies from Chapters One and Two to identify one to two areas where you have improvement ideas. Make sure these are areas you care about and where you believe you can truly make a difference.
   ○ Use strategies from Chapters Three and Four to evaluate which of your ideas has the best chance of gaining support from your managers, peers, customers, and stakeholders.

○ Identify and improve vulnerable areas of your concept and enhance your idea's strengths.

2. **Communicating and Gaining Buy-In:** (Chapters Four through Six)

○ Discuss your idea informally with key players to better understand the benefits, opportunities, concerns, and risks they perceive.

○ Mitigate concerns and risks and maximize opportunities and benefits.

○ Quantify and communicate the benefits of your initiative over the status quo and other alternatives. If helpful, consider the Opportunity Model (Chapter Six) to compare options.

3. **Implementation and Making an Impact:** (Chapters Seven through Ten)

○ Consider the most relevant implementation strategies (Chapter Eight) for your initiative.

○ Be aware of potential risks and opportunities that may occur during implementation.

○ Understand reasons new initiatives fail to achieve objectives and prepare accordingly.

○ To reduce risk concerns, consider pilot testing your concept. Stay alert for any unintended consequences. Learn and improve upon your original idea.

○ Seek feedback and constructive criticism and respond accordingly.

○ Be alert for additional spin-off benefits and the potential to build upon your initial success.

○ Measure your progress and impact.

Summary

You *CAN* do this! It's up to you to "make it real!"

The Impact of Individuals: Never underestimate the potential impact determined and passionate individuals can make on a work group, organization, or community. *Unauthorized Progress* includes stories of individual leaders, at all levels, encountered during my professional career. There are tens of thousands of similar stories about proactive people taking initiative and making significant, positive contributions; people willing and committed to leading from the middle. Consider what you can do to initiate or influence positive change in your organization.

The Impact of Teams: Teams of individuals with a common purpose and dedicated to a specific goal can be extraordinarily effective in leading or influencing change. Wisdom is gained through candid discussion and debate of various assumptions, approaches, and shared experiences, and a variety of backgrounds and expertise can be key to success. This was critical to the Coast Guard teams working to improve maritime domain awareness who produced a capability valued at $140 million. The combination of operational experience, data management, information technology, and satellite communications expertise created a unique collective skill set that enabled the team to succeed.

The Impact on Organizations: As proactive individuals and teams take the initiative to improve performance, they can have a positive impact on the entire organization. The positive "virus" of *leading from the middle* can infect the whole organization, leading people to be more proactive and take initiative, rather than waiting for management to tell them what to do and when to do it. In the process, people are happier in their work and more committed to their organization and its mission.

The startup of the Coast Guard Innovation Program demonstrates how organizations can create a supportive environment that encourages their people to stretch themselves to reach their potential. Such organizations not only achieve improved performance, but their people also have significantly increased job satisfaction and commitment. As a result, they stay and have more sustained focus on accomplishing their mission. Another benefit is fewer job vacancies, reduced hiring needs, and lower training costs due to fewer new employees being hired. During crisis situations, organizations that encourage an innovative spirit and empower their workforce are more likely to resolve tough new problems they encounter, such as the Coast Guard's highly effective responses during Hurricane Katrina and the Deepwater Horizon oil spill.

The Collective Impact: If multiple organizations could develop and encourage an empowering approach to their workforce, collaboration and interagency cooperation could greatly increase. We could make progress on serious issues negatively impacting our nation and the world such as poverty, national debt, starvation and famine, and eradication of diseases. While *wicked challenges* such as these are extremely complex, we have the potential to make a truly significant contribution toward solving them.

The Impact on *YOU*: But most important, what is the impact on you, if you follow the strategies presented in this book to take initiative and be proactive? The Coast Guard innovators were more engaged, more energized, and had much greater job satisfaction. The impact of adopting an attitude of *leading from the middle* may mean you look forward to each day because you know your efforts are making a difference; you're making a positive contribution that truly matters.

Next *UP*:

Answer the Call to Action: Make a difference and a positive impact by taking initiative to proactively *lead from the middle*! Review the chapters most relevant to your situation, consider the strategies described, and use those that may help. Consider sharing this book with a family member, friend, or like-minded colleague you'd like to help succeed. Spread the concepts, ideas, knowledge, and strategies for effectively *leading from the middle* (LFM). Help the LFM community grow! Help yourself, and others, achieve desired goals and potential and feel good about doing it.

Let me know your stories and results! I can be contacted at www. linkedin.com/geoffrey-abbott/.

> *Life is short, break the rules, forgive quickly, kiss slowly, love truly, laugh uncontrollably, and never regret anything that made you smile. Twenty years from now you will be more disappointed by the things you didn't do than by the ones you did.*
> *~ Mark Twain*

ACKNOWLEDGMENTS

This book would not, could not come together without the input, stories, and feedback from so many friends, colleagues, and family members. The collective experience of these friends and colleagues in the Coast Guard, military, first responder community, good government and leadership development fields amounts to centuries of expertise. I'm in their debt for their stories, lessons learned, best practices, and innovative solutions as they lead *from the middle* and serve as role models to countless others.

I want to thank my family, Lisa and our two sons, Matthew and Nick, for their patience and countless hours offering and challenging book concepts and ideas, proofreading, and providing the constructive criticism necessary to make this book relevant and useful for current and future leaders. Lisa, my loving wife of forty-one years, including twenty-eight as a military spouse, helped me identify the most valuable lessons learned and best practices readers can emulate for their own success. I had assumed most organizations supported their people working to improve their teams and organization, but Lisa pointed out that this wasn't always the case. Her observation led me to write an additional chapter on "Death Valley Strategies," what to do when facing a difficult work environment/culture and leaving isn't an immediate option. I've learned from both our sons of the challenges they face trying to *lead from the middle* at the start of their careers: Matthew conducting architecture work with private sector firms and Nick starting his career as a federal public servant. Both have learned and shared their stories of good and bad leaders and together, we've strategized how to help them and their organizations be successful. Some of their lessons learned and strategies are included in this book.

I'm immensely grateful for the many people who've helped shape my thoughts and actions on leadership over the decades. I especially want to acknowledge the following leaders who gave me invaluable leadership insights and inspired me: Captain Bob Kuehnl, USCG (Retired), Captain Gary Frago, USCG (Retired), Captain Larry Brudnicki, USCG (Retired), Ray Blunt (my Excellence in Government Fellows coach), Admiral Thad Allen, USCG (Retired), and Mark Nishan (Instructor/facilitator and colleague at the SEC's College of Leadership Development), I'm forever in your debt. As my Excellence in Government Fellows coach, Ray nurtured my interest and passion for leading from the middle and encouraged me to explore it further which led to the creation of this book.

Likewise, I've learned valuable lessons on challenging perceived boundaries and often moving beyond them from many colleagues I've been honored to work besides including: Mike Clark (electrical technician), Ted Dernago (real property specialist), the entire Coast Guard Civil Engineering Unit Providence team (fifty-five awesome civilian and military members), and Captain Karl Calvo, USCG (Retired). I am also very thankful for Dr. Marie Westbrook, the first Dean of the Securities and Exchange Commission's College of Leadership Development, who took a chance on hiring me despite having little teaching experience after I completed my doctoral work.

I'm blessed to know many of the heroes in this book personally, those involved in many of the inspiring stories of *leading from the middle* to make meaningful impacts. Many are Coast Guard Innovation Award winners, Excellence in Government Fellows, and just ordinary public servants who are truly extraordinary and effectively lead from the middle. In particular, I want to thank Lieutenant Commander Chris Kluckhuhn, USCGR (Retired), Colonel Steve "Hoog" Hoogasian, USAF (Retired), Matt Kern (federal contractor extraordinaire), "Dan" (military advisor), Lieutenant Commander Lil Maizer, USCG

(Retired), Danny Prosser, Captain Jan Stevens, USCG (Retired), and Luke Dlhopolsky. My apologies to anyone I failed to mention! You know the impact you've had, and our nation is better for your contributions!

I would also like to thank my trusted readers, who contributed their best thoughts and ideas for improving the initial manuscript. Their support and suggestions make this book more valuable and useful for current and future practitioners leading change. In addition to those already mentioned, my trusted readers also include Commander Jon Heller, USCG (Retired) (Director of the Admiral James Loy Leadership Institute), Scott Winter (international executive coach and motivational coach), Kitty Wooley (EIG Senior Fellow and Leadership Board member; founder of Excellence in Government Fellows & Friends), Ellen Metcalf (faculty, Admiral James Loy Leadership Institute), Jackye Zimmermann (EIG Senior Fellow and Leadership Board member, Founder of Conversations with Leaders), Sheldon Lehrner (EIG Senior Fellow and Leadership Board Member), Walt Besecker (EIG Fellows Coach), Carol Scanelli, USA (retired and federal employee), Ilyse Veron (editor, former Reporter for MacNeil-Lehrer Report), Lieutenant Colonel Anita Springer, USAF (Retired), and Lieutenant Colonel Cheryl Brown, USAF (Retired).

Producing a high-quality book from an initial manuscript requires skill, knowledge, and professional guidance, especially if you're writing your first book. I'm very fortunate and grateful for the guidance and advice of my "book shepherd," Diana M. Needham, who provided me with the steps necessary to publish this book and to my editor, Lisbeth Tanz, whose insights and suggestions resulted in a better, clearer book for my readers. Thanks also to Maria-Alaina Rambus for her graphic design assistance for the book. Your collective contributions transformed a passionate idea to help develop leaders into a high-quality book that can serve as a valuable resource for enhancing the effectiveness of current and future leaders at all levels.

A Special Gift from Geoff

Now that you have read *Unauthorized Progress – Leading From the Middle*, you are equipped with the tools and strategies needed to effectively initiate and influence positive change in your organization or community and make meaningful impacts. As you apply the techniques described, you will develop increased confidence to tackle complex challenges and issues that matter to you, your team, and your organization.

I also created the *Unauthorized Progress (UP)* toolkit to make it easy for you to immediately apply leading from the middle strategies. It includes summaries of key topics and useful tools:

- Leading Change from the Middle process flowchart
- Criteria decision-makers use to evaluate initiatives
- Common reasons innovative ideas are not pursued
- Leading from the middle implementation strategies and when they are most effective
- Reasons change initiatives fail and mitigation strategies
- Templates you can copy and adapt for your personal initiatives:
  - ○ SWOT Analysis, Importance versus Urgency matrix, Cause and Effect diagram
- Sample questions to engage stakeholders and learn their perspectives

While the *UP Toolkit* can be purchased, I'm making it available free to all readers to accelerate your ability to lead from wherever you are in your organization.

Go to http://GeoffAbbottLeadership.com/gift to register for your gift. As another gift you will also receive tips and further information from me to confidently lead *from the middle*. You may, of course, unsubscribe at any time.

I'm in your corner. Let me know if I can help further – you can do this!

Geoff

Geoff holds a Doctorate in Business Administration, conducting research to improve organizational performance through innovation and empowering the workforce, earned two MIT engineering graduate degrees, and a Bachelor of Science degree from the U.S. Coast Guard Academy. A Professional Engineer, Geoff served as a national director of the Society of American Military Engineers (SAME) and is a founding director of MIT's Military Alumni Association.

Awards and honors include the Legion of Merit, Meritorious Service Medal (four), CG Commendation Medal (two), EIG Senior Fellows Community Award, Analytic Services' Platt Award for Authors, SEC's Veterans Charity Award, and SAME's Academy of Fellows.

Learn more about Geoff and/or contact him on LinkedIn at https://www.linkedin.com/in/geoffrey-abbott/.

ABOUT THE AUTHOR

Dr. Geoff Abbott is the senior faculty member at the Securities and Exchange Commission's College of Leadership Development (CLD), responsible for development, delivery, and oversight of SEC leadership programs.

Prior to joining CLD, Geoff was a thirty-year career Coast Guard officer where he held two commands, led the Performance Excellence Program, chaired the Commandant's Innovation Council, and served as the first CG/DHS Fellow at the Homeland Security Institute.

As an Excellence in Government (EIG) Senior Fellow, EIG co-coach and Partnership for Public Service Leadership Alumni Board member (seventeen years), he's led several workshops on leading change *from the middle*.